AN END TIME PROPHETIC
WAKE UP CALL

BEYOND
EARTHLY
REALMS

AN END TIME PROPHETIC
WAKE UP CALL

BEYOND
EARTHLY
REALMS

JASON CARTER

TRUMPET BLAST PUBLISHING

And it shall come to pass afterward that I will
pour out My Spirit on all flesh;
Your sons and your daughters shall prophesy,
Your old men shall dream dreams,
Your young men shall see visions.

Joel 2:28 NKJV

And behold, I am coming quickly,
and My reward is with Me, to give to every one
according to his work. I am the Alpha and the
Omega, the Beginning and the End,
the First and the Last.

Revelation 22:12-13 NKJV

And the Spirit and the bride say, Come!
And let him who hears say, Come!
And let him who thirsts come. Whoever desires,
let him take the water of life freely.

Revelation 22:17 NKJV

This book is dedicated To:

My darling wife Orsola, who is a tower of spiritual strength, and without whom I could never have written this book;

My father and mother, David and Christine, who without their exemplary Christian example and faithfulness to God I would not know the Lord Jesus today;

Colin Blackman, the pastor of the church I grew up in, who during my childhood and teens greatly inspired me to fulfil God's call on my life;

My old boss Francis Newing, who I had the privilege of spending many hours over the years talking together about the things of God;

Lastly, but most certainly, not least…

My Lord and Saviour Jesus Christ, who brought me out of darkness and into His marvellous light, and without whom I would be absolutely lost forever!

Contents

Introduction

My dear friend,

It is such an honour for me that you are taking the time to read my book *Beyond Earthly Realms.*

Here in these pages you will find a detailed account of an approximately ten hour vision experience I had while I was awake in the day, followed by other visionary experiences and night dream visions, all of which I experienced between October 1991—January 1992. In addition, I have included some other accounts from different times. Before now I have not shared these experiences with anyone except my wife, and more recently my brother and sister-in-law. The time was not right. In fact I didn't think I would ever disclose them until I experienced a dream vision back in October 2009 and felt the urging of the Holy Spirit to make the vision available to all who would choose to read it in these last days.

As you read about these visions you may wonder to yourself how on earth I came to receive them. You may also find the whole subject of visions, dreams and angelic visitations to be fascinating in itself.

I need therefore to stress two things. Firstly, I would like to say that in making these experiences publicly available it is not my aim in any way to draw attention to myself. God forbid! John the Baptist, while considering the nature of his high calling which was to prepare the way for the Messiah, could have chosen to boast that he was somebody special. But he said, *"He must increase, but I must decrease."* (John 3:30)

Likewise the apostle Paul, who received exceedingly great revelations that enabled him to write much of the New Testament, said of himself, *"For I am the least worthy of all the apostles."* (1 Corinthians 15:9)

If these great men of God who received sublime revelations and were chosen for such lofty tasks considered themselves so insignificant, then how much more should we?

This humbling of oneself in the light of the glory of God and in the face of mankind must always be a priority in our Christian lives. We are servants of all, not lords over others. Indeed let us not forget that even the sinless Son of God Jesus Christ, who daily walked in divine revelation, became a servant to his disciples. Again, how much more should we humble ourselves?

Secondly, by writing this book it is not my purpose to draw attention to these experiences as though they are something more important than they actually are. I have never spent any time seeking after these things. My heart's cry and deep longing has always been to draw up alongside God and to be with Him in the beauty of His holiness. A truly inspiring verse on this subject is found in Exodus 33. It describes when Moses met with the Lord. It says in verse 11, *"So the Lord spoke to Moses face to face, as a man speaks to his friend."* Wow! What a wonderful accolade for Moses! Can you imagine it? God spoke with Moses just like a friend! They shared each other's hearts. God disclosed what was on His mind to Moses! That's what I want daily.

My friend, we can all have this daily. He is just waiting to spend time with us!

All this highlights how we must have a biblical perspective on the place these supernatural phenomena have in our Christian experience. If we do not, we are in danger of losing sight of Christ and falling into error. We will start pursuing supernatural phenomena instead of the person of God. This will culminate in us boasting in our experiences rather than the Lord, in the gifts rather than the Giver of the gifts.

Furthermore, the apostle Paul exhorts us to understand that great revelations are of no value without a certain divine quality at work in the life of the one who receives them. He writes:

If I had the gift of prophecy and knew all about what is going to happen in the future, knew everything about everything, but didn't love others, what good would it do? Even if I had the gift of faith so that I could speak to a mountain and make it move, I would still be worth nothing at all without love. If I gave everything I have to poor people, and if I were burned alive for preaching the Gospel but didn't love others, it would be of no value whatever. (1 Corinthians 13:2-3, TLB)

See here the emphasis Paul puts on love over prophecy? Notice also below how he relegates prophecy and revelation into a much lesser position. Prophecy he says will *not* continue but love will continue forever. So let us consume ourselves in acquiring and exhibiting this eternal love!

Here's what Paul says about it:

Love is very patient and kind, never jealous or envious, never boastful or proud, never haughty or selfish or rude. Love does not demand its own way. It is not irritable or touchy. It does not hold grudges and will hardly even notice when others do it wrong. It is never glad about injustice, but rejoices whenever truth wins out. If you love someone, you will be loyal to him no matter what the cost. You will always believe in him, always expect the best of him, and always stand your ground in defending him.

All the special gifts and powers from God will someday come to an end, but love goes on forever. Someday prophecy and speaking in unknown languages and special knowledge—these gifts will disappear. Now we know so little, even with our special gifts, and the preaching of those most gifted is still so poor. But when we have been made perfect and complete, then the need for these inadequate special gifts will come to an end, and they will disappear.

There are three things that remain—faith, hope, and love—and the greatest of these is love (1 Corinthians 13:4-10, 13 TLB).

Without the love that comes from having an intimate friendship with Jesus Christ, prophetic visions and dreams can become worthless and worse still can cause harm to the soul, as they tend to draw the heart away from Christ rather than towards Him.

Indeed let us also remember that when we receive such revelations from heaven, as sublime as they sometimes may be, they have no saving quality of themselves!

Revelation 19:10 tells us plainly that 'the testimony of Jesus is the spirit of prophecy'. Note: the verse says the testimony of Jesus not the testimony of the experience. If the Spirit of Christ Jesus does not reside within the prophecy then it is not prophecy at all! In fact without the presence of Christ, prophecy puffs up and boasts. It is only the One who was born of a virgin, died on that cruel cross for our wrongdoings, who rose from the dead on the third day and who will come again to judge the living and the dead on the last day, who is glorified in true prophecy.

Prophecy does not save us and neither does it have the capacity to make us any more righteous. Jesus alone saves. Jesus spoke about those who thought that because they prophesied and performed wonders that they were saved. But Jesus showed the value these things have on their own. He said many will come on that day saying, did we not prophecy in your name? But he will say, 'away from me I never knew you!' (Matthew 7:23).

In 2009 I received an angelic visitation. Of all the things I could have imagined in that moment as the angel stood before me

— poised to utter a message from the Lord which he had, by the way, travelled thousands of miles to speak to me — I could never have imagined the word that would come forth from his lips. As he gently placed his hand upon my heart he uttered one single word "LOVE". That was it! And then he vanished.

That one word message 'love' from the Lord was multi-faceted for me. One of those facets was this, that without the divine love that proceeds from the Father into our hearts, all our Christian activity counts for absolutely nothing. This divine love is not ordinary love. It is a love that arrests our hearts to the point that it continuously bubbles up and flows up and out of our lives, and into the lives of others. It is a love that is captivated with a passionate affection for God, who himself is love! It even proceeds from us, and enables us to love our enemies with all our hearts! Imagine that! Oh that we would be consumed by this love!

So friends, let us not seek after supernatural phenomena in the belief that these experiences somehow bestow a special authority upon us. It is for reasons of power that Pagans seek after such things. But rather let us pursue Jesus Christ in whom the greatest gift of love is to be found, and then walk in that love. As the hymn writer calls it, *'love divine all loves excelling!'*

Yes, let us also, as the apostle Paul writes, eagerly desire all spiritual gifts and especially prophecy (1 Corinthians 14:1). But let divine love be our first and highest goal! Prophecy, dreams, visions, and angelic visitations flow out of our intimate union with Christ — not the other way around.

So what is the purpose of making these visions available for everyone to read today?

Firstly, it is to glorify the God of heaven and to reveal His Son Jesus Christ to anyone, believer or unbeliever, who reads these pages.

Secondly, it is my prayer that it will set all who read it free —

free from fear, and free from pain and suffering in the light of Jesus, drawing the reader into an ever closer union with Him.

Thirdly, it is my prayer that all who read it will hear the cry of Jesus Christ who stands at the door and knocks, that it will prepare all who read it for things soon coming upon the earth, that it will prepare hearts to meet Him in death, or to meet Him through his glorious and second appearing when He comes on the clouds of heaven.

May God bless you and touch you as you read!

Love in Christ Jesus,

Jason

Part I

The Revelation

Chapter 1

Journey into the Heavens

Chapter 1

Journey into the Heavens

t was an ordinary morning in October 1991 when it happened.

The associate pastor from my old church had telephoned me earlier that morning at the Christian graphics and print studio where I worked and asked if he could have some tracts that I had co-written with my boss. These leaflets warned against the dangers of being involved with various religious movements including, among others, New Age groups, Freemasonry and the Occult.

A few minutes later I opened the double doors and stepped into the church.

As I climbed the long stairway to the main meeting area, what felt like a small electrical charge began to run through my entire body. As it did I became aware of an increasing sense of danger all around me, I was convinced something terrible was about to happen.

I nervously continued to climb the stairs as the electrical charge intensified. The sense of impending danger grew stronger with every step. When I reached the top I opened the door to the main meeting area and as I entered I became totally enveloped in what I can only describe as a thick electrical energy which coursed all over my body from the top of my head, around my face, all the way down to the tip of my toes.

I approached the stage area at the front of the church. Electricity was now pulsing over me with an incredible strength.

I began to stagger. The weight of whatever was on me was too great.

Inevitably I fell to my knees.

The senior and associate pastors helped me to a chair and I sat between them, the energy still consuming my body in ever increasing power.

The Dark Rock

The physical realm now began to fade away in a whitish haze. To me it no longer seemed real. It felt like it was all only a figment of my imagination. It was the spiritual realm that appeared real and in full focus.

I was now taken beyond the earthly, physical realm into an altogether different reality.

I saw the heavens opened before me and I found myself standing in the air, as though suspended with no ground beneath me.

There I stood in the deep blue space amongst the stars of the heavens looking out into eternity.

As I remained suspended in the air, I heard the deafening and continuous noise of what sounded like the blast of a trumpet. It could be heard all around.

I looked upwards and saw something that resembled a gigantic dark rock — like a vast boulder — hurtling with incredible speed towards the earth. The rock looked like a star falling from the heavens. Its essence was utterly evil. The rock hit the earth with a sudden and devastating impact.

The earth shuddered and responded as though in terrible

agony. The place where the rock had landed was Europe. I let out a piercing and terrible cry of pain. Somehow I knew in my spirit that something demonic had come to Europe and I felt the searing pain of the impact myself.

A Christ-Consumed People

Immediately afterwards I moved location and saw the Holy Spirit residing in the hearts of the true saints of God. This was a source of great joy and comfort to my soul. The Holy Spirit was not just present with these people. He literally embodied them.

The eyes of these saints were so consumed with the indwelling presence of the Holy Spirit that they glowed with what appeared to be the eyes of Christ himself.

Their eyes were connected directly to their spirits. Christ was visible in their eyes because He resided so deeply in the spirits of these fully surrendered Christians.

These people walked as though in slow motion throughout the earth — gently, humbly and gracefully showing Jesus Christ to the world in good deeds.

Some were silent and inconspicuous, while others were more vocal and obvious.

Each was as vital as the other.

There was no division between male and female, or between those of great rank and those of lesser rank.

All this felt totally out of place and irrelevant among these Christ-consumed people.

The Golden Tower

I staggered to my feet in a state of wonder. The earthly realm was still distant to me, as if it was a mere thought in my mind.

With the energy still running through my body from my head

to my toes, I was suddenly taken to another place. This time I found myself kneeling on the ground in a desert, my knees in the sand that was all around me.

I saw a giant, cylindrical, gold tower before me. It felt as if it had the spirit of man in it as it grew taller and taller before me. I watched as brick by brick the tower was assembled at an incredible pace, and as it grew taller and taller I ascended with it, flying up and up with every round of golden bricks that was laid in quick succession.

Suddenly the tower came to an abrupt stop as it was completed.

I now found myself hovering at the top of the tower which had ascended far above the clouds.

I saw that the tower which now embodied the collective spirits of many people — an indecipherable number — had become like God. I was totally perplexed by this and did not understand what it meant.

The vision then began to subside a little and the energy at work in my body lessened in intensity.

I left the church building trying to compose myself.

I walked through the town centre, my flesh still tingling from the experience.

The Redeemed of God

As I walked through the streets the earthly realm still seemed distant to me and the heavenly realm more present and real before my eyes.

Now however, I was walking in the spirit through the earth after the rapture of the saints and after the coming of the Lord Jesus.

The people walking around me were clothed in bright white garments right down to their feet.

They moved about as though in slow motion and it looked to

me as if they were not walking but rather gliding two or three inches above the ground. I wasn't sure exactly how they moved.

These people were in total peace and contentment, with clear hearts and minds. They did not look either to the left or the right but appeared to be fixing their gaze straight ahead. They seemed to me to be engaged in some kind of task but I had no idea what this was.

These were the redeemed of God, whose garments had been washed in the precious blood of Jesus.

The New Jerusalem

As I turned the corner I looked up beyond the people and I saw in the horizon far away what appeared to be the Holy City of God in the sky. The New Jerusalem was descending down out of the heavens with a great light as of the sun. This light was emanating from within it. The city itself gave the light. There was no sun to illuminate it. The light was golden.

Indeed, the city itself appeared to be made of gold. Near the centre of the city, which seemed symmetrical in design, a great golden domed building stood majestic and tall above the rest and glistened in its own light.

The Trinity

Directly after this I witnessed something that is very hard to explain with our earth-bound vocabulary. I experienced the union of the Blessed Trinity — The Father, The Son and The Holy Spirit.

I didn't see their individual forms but I felt their presence in a deeply intimate way — up close, as though in front of my face, as close as a friend is to a friend.

It was as though I saw the Blessed Trinity — The Father, The Son and The Holy Spirit and I was somehow in complete and direct fellowship with them and that it appeared perfectly natural to be so.

It didn't feel like anything out of the ordinary.

I was quite at ease.

The three persons of the Trinity were happy that I was present with them. Their oneness with each other was so complete.

They appeared to me like crystal clear blue water that contained countless thoughts — a swirling expanse in which the Father, the Son and the Holy Spirit spoke with one another continuously and without end.

My finite, human mind was unable to contain the extremely intense sensation that was now passing through it.

It appeared to me I was being so totally submerged and saturated that I was no longer able to contain the experience within my mind.

It felt like I was somehow drowning in it but I was not in any way fearful.

This meeting with God flooded my mind.

I was experiencing what felt like a torrent, and I held on for dear life, lest I might be swept away by this great and wonderful experience and lose myself in it forever.

In essence I witnessed the One True God as three individual persons, but yet they were ONE and the SAME!

This was an unfathomable and glorious mystery to me.

Godly Sorrow

Later I became greatly grieved in my spirit as I considered myself not worthy of entering into such a union with the Lord.

It seemed to me that this was no place at all for mortal man to dwell and so I felt sorrowful in my spirit.

Years earlier when I was around twelve years of age I had

received a vision that had resulted in similar feelings.

I had been reading the Bible with earnest while lying in my bed one night. I just could not put the Bible down and was captivated by the story of Solomon building the temple of the Lord. I kept on reading chapter after chapter because I was sure I was about to come across something through which God was going to speak to me.

Before I fell asleep I had a vision of the Lord Jesus Christ in clouds of smoke sitting upon His throne in heaven. Encircling Him were angels blowing long golden trumpets.

No sooner had I seen this than I fell into a deep sleep upon my Bible.

On awakening the following morning I had no immediate memory of the vision that had taken place the night before. But now I felt afraid and uneasy in my spirit, as if there was an evil presence in my bedroom.

I just knew I had to jump out of bed and get out of my room as quickly as possible.

As soon as I did, my sense of peace returned. But on returning to my room I experienced the same uneasiness once again, as though I should not be in there.

I questioned myself. Why was I experiencing such feelings of anguish when the day before and all other days for that matter I had felt fine? Then it dawned on me that posters of a certain music band I had been following with teenage fervency were all over my room, even parts of the ceiling. I realized this group had become an idol to me.

At that moment I understood that God was jealous for me; He wanted to have me for His very own. He did not want to share me with another, not because He was possessive and selfish, but because He loved me, just as a husband loves his wife and does not want to share her with another. This is what the first and second of the Ten Commandments teaches. Both commandments were born out of His passionate and affectionate love for us.

'You shall have no other gods before Me, and You shall not make for yourself an idol in the form of anything.' (Exodus 20)

Such was the distress in my spirit that I had grieved the Lord's heart through my lack of faithfulness that I frantically ripped down and destroyed all the posters in my bedroom.

Holy, Holy, Holy

Soon after doing this I left the house to go to school. On returning home that evening I explained to my parents that the previous night I had been reading the Scriptures, and that I was unable to put the Bible down until I eventually fell asleep on it. I told them how that morning I had felt compelled to remove all my posters.

At this point I still hadn't recalled the vision I had seen before falling asleep.

I sat down in the armchair and picked up the Bible and began to read to my parents from the place where I had left off. It was 2 Chronicles 7:1-3:

When Solomon finished praying, fire flashed down from heaven and burned up the burnt offerings and sacrifices, and the glorious presence of the Lord filled the Temple. The priests could not enter the Temple of the Lord because the glorious presence of the Lord filled it. When all the people of Israel saw the fire coming down and the glorious presence of the Lord filling the Temple, they fell face down on the ground and worshiped and praised the Lord, saying, "He is good! His faithful love endures forever!"

As I read I suddenly became aware again of the strong presence of the Lord.

The Lord approached slowly from behind and round to the left side of my face, like a shadow. I could feel what the Lord was feeling. He was very still and calm and intensely serious.

In terror I threw the Bible onto the living room floor and leapt out of the armchair, hiding myself in the corner of the room where I wept. I curled myself up in a ball with my hands covering my ears and head in an attempt to shield myself from the Lord's presence.

The vision I had received the night before was now replaying vividly in my mind, as though it had been triggered by the words I had just read aloud from 2 Chronicles 7.

The presence of the Lord was so intense and awesome that I felt completely naked and sinful in His Holy, Holy, Holy sight, and I wept with anguish that the Lord had come to meet with a sinner such as me.

What I had just read from 2 Chronicles — and had failed to get around to reading the night before — was the vision I had seen of the glory of the Lord filling the temple. Like the people of Israel in that story, I had fallen to the ground and worshipped the Lord.

A Consuming Fire

When Isaiah saw the glory of the Lord filling the temple he exclaimed, 'I am ruined! For I am a man of unclean lips.'

Here is the passage from Isaiah 6:1-7 (NIV):

I saw the Lord, high and exalted, seated on a throne; and the train of his robe filled the temple. Above him were seraphim, each with six wings: With two wings they covered their faces, with two they covered their feet, and with two they were flying. And they were calling to one another: 'Holy, holy, holy is the Lord Almighty; the whole earth is full of his glory.'

At the sound of their voices the doorposts and thresholds shook and the temple was filled with smoke.

'Woe to me!' I cried. 'I am ruined! For I am a man of unclean lips, and I live among a people of unclean lips, and my eyes have seen the King, the Lord Almighty.'

Then one of the seraphim flew to me with a live coal in his hand, which he had taken with tongs from the altar. With it he touched my mouth and said, 'See, this has touched your lips; your guilt is taken away and your sin atoned for...'

After having seen the Lord in all His holiness and glory Isaiah cried, 'Woe to me — I am ruined' — or, in another translation, 'I am undone!'

This is what happens to a person when they come into contact with the gloriously bright presence of the Lord in all His Holiness and Splendour.

The Bible says that 'our God is a consuming fire' (Hebrews 12:29).

In the Old Testament we read that fire came out from the presence of the LORD and consumed the people and they died before the LORD (Leviticus 10:2).

The fullness and intensity of His Holy presence can consume us in an instant!

Jesus Changes Everything

We should always remember how the LORD struck Uzzah dead because he touched the ark of the covenant (the holy presence of God) in order to steady it (1 Chronicles 13:10).

We should also always remember that Jehovah is still the same awesome God today and that sinful man and a holy God do not mix. The Bible is explicit regarding God's unchangeable character; there is no shadow of turning in Him.

James 1:17 talks about *'[God]...who does not change like shifting shadows'* (NIV).

In Psalm 102:27 we read, *'you remain the same.'*

While again the LORD declares in Malachi 3:6, *'I the LORD do not change.'*

So if the Lord God Jehovah does not change, and He is forever holy, how can we who are sinful ever hope to come into an intimate communion and relationship with Him without feeling wretched or, worse still, dying in His presence?

What can change this unchanging reality?

Remember how the angel flew to Isaiah when he was confessing that he was ruined? The angel touched Isaiah's lips with a burning coal and declared that his guilt was taken away, his sin forgiven!

The prophet Jeremiah foretold the change that was going to come upon us and referred to it as a new covenant.

'Behold, the days are coming, says the Lord, when I will make a new covenant with the house of Israel and with the house of Judah — not according to the covenant that I made with their fathers in the day that I took them by the hand to lead them out of the land of Egypt, My covenant which they broke, though I was a husband to them, says the Lord. But this is the covenant that I will make with the house of Israel after those days, says the Lord: I will put My law in their minds, and write it on their hearts; and I will be their God, and they shall be My people. No more shall every man teach his neighbour, and every man his brother, saying, 'Know the Lord,' for they all shall know Me, from the least of them to the greatest of them, says the Lord. For I will forgive their iniquity, and their sin I will remember no more.'

Jeremiah 31:31-34 (NKJV)

These words pointed to the coming of the Messiah Jesus.

So Jesus Christ brought about the change!

He was the fulfilment of the prophecies of Jeremiah and others.

Jesus spoke of this new covenant when He instituted the Lord's

Supper. He said, *'This is My body which is given for you; do this in remembrance of Me,'* and, *'This cup is the new covenant in My blood, which is shed for you.'* (Luke 22:19-20, NKJV)

Not Guilty!

What a wonderfully kind God we serve. He is full of love and compassion! He does not hold our sinfulness against us as He rightly should. He does not leave us ruined, undone or naked and trembling in fear as we deserve. The Lord God in unbridled generosity and unbounded love sent us His only Son Jesus Christ to provide the pardon for our guilt and sin! And in the most astounding miracle of all he declares us 'not guilty!' by freeing us from our bondage to sin and bringing us back into an intimate and close relationship with Him.

The writer of Hebrews summed this up when he declared:

'For you have not come to the mountain that may be touched and that burned with fire, and to blackness and darkness and tempest, and the sound of a trumpet and the voice of words, so that those who heard it begged that the word should not be spoken to them anymore. (For they could not endure what was commanded: "And if so much as a beast touches the mountain, it shall be stoned or shot with an arrow." And so terrifying was the sight that Moses said, "I am exceedingly afraid and trembling.") But you have come to Mount Zion and to the city of the living God, the heavenly Jerusalem, to an innumerable company of angels, to the general assembly and church of the firstborn who are registered in heaven, to God the Judge of all, to the spirits of just men made perfect, to Jesus the Mediator of the new covenant, and to the blood of sprinkling that speaks better things than that of Abel.' (Hebrews 12:18-24)

Jesus is the mediator of the new covenant!

He brought about the change!

Chapter 2

A Brave New Church

Chapter 2

A Brave New Church

We now return to the vision I received in October 1991. By now it was afternoon and I was still deeply affected by the vision I'd had of the Trinity. I went back to work to speak with my boss Francis, a wonderful man of God. He attended the Methodist church just out of town.

I said, 'it feels as if the spiritual realm is more real than the physical.'

I did not give a reason. Nor did I describe what I had seen.

But he looked at me straight in the eyes.

'What you've had is a Damascus Road experience,' he said, clearly influenced by the Holy Spirit. He was making reference to the story in Acts Chapter 9 of the encounter that Saul of Tarsus had with the Risen Jesus. This was while he was on his way to Damascus to persecute the followers of Jesus. The vision had temporarily blinded Saul and turned out to be life-changing for him. Saul was renamed Paul and turned from being a persecutor of Christians to a preacher of the Good News.

I left the office, unable to do any more work.

Somehow I managed to walk from the town centre back to my home.

Thirty minutes later I walked through the front door and into the dining room, where both my parents were standing. Within a few moments I needed to sit down. The same powerful sensation of electrical energy was pulsating around my body once again.

A Vision of the Cross

Once I was seated at the dining room table I re-entered the spiritual realm.

I found myself racing at an unbelievable speed through a long tunnel that twisted and turned. It appeared to be slowly descending. The walls looked as if they were a thick dark cloud with many shades of grey, ranging from a nearly white colour to pitch black.

Suddenly I was out the other end and found myself standing suspended in mid air above the Cross at Calvary, as though transported back in time.

I looked around in a state of astonishment and shock. Part of me was afraid that I would never be able to return to my own time. But mostly I felt confused. How was it that I was now present at one of the most terrible and yet sacred events in history?

As I looked down, I realised that I had exactly the same vantage point as Christ himself. He was suspended and cruelly transfixed in a standing position on the Cross, looking down at his surroundings. It felt to me as if I was looking through my precious Saviour's eyes.

Everything seemed grey to me — no colour at all, only shades of grey.

Clouds and smoke seemed to be billowing about Golgotha's hill, swirling and twisting all around me in the air.

I slowly turned my gaze to the left and then to the right, looking at the outstretched arms of my Saviour — the arms that had brought so much comfort and healing to so many.

His muscles were taut.

His skin was pale, as though his flesh had been drained of blood.

As I gazed through the Saviour's eyes, my soul was filled with an immense and overwhelming sorrow.

I felt what He felt — the grief that He was enduring and the appalling and repulsive sin of the world that He was bearing.

In my heart I knew with crushing certainty that every wicked deed committed from the beginning of time to that dreadful day was laid upon His shoulders.

The one who had never sinned was carrying our sin.

He was carrying my sin.

The House of David

After a few heart beats the vision faded and I was no longer at Calvary.

It was now early evening and I had gone upstairs to my bedroom. The spiritual realm still felt more real to me than the physical.

Within a few moments I found myself transported to a new location. I was staring into the great and dark expanse of the heavens when a cry began to emerge from deep within my heart. It was a name.

'David! David! David!' I shouted.

As I spoke this name in some anguish of soul, I felt a pain in my right side.

I clutched my side in agony.

As I did, I saw the lifeless body of the Saviour laying on the ground. A Roman legionary had moments earlier, thrust the blade of his spear into the Lord's side. It was as if he had pierced me as well. As I felt the pain, I was sorely distressed and grieved in my spirit that the Saviour's body had been so mistreated and abused.

Once again I cried out.

'David! David! David!'

As I continued to shout, I saw in the deepest and remotest darkness of the heavens an extraordinary house emerge. It was gleaming with gold and encircled by swirling and radiant clouds of glory.

I went on uttering the name, 'David,' my voice becoming softer and less urgent as I gazed upon this wondrous site.

Then I understood: this was the House of David — the house from which Christ himself was descended.

I was filled with awe.

The house was small, but beautiful and majestic.

Then I saw generations of Jewish and Gentile people filing out from this far away house and proceeding in two separate lines through the heavens until they reached the place where the resurrected Christ was standing, clothed in white with arms outstretched.

When all these peoples reached Christ they then parted and stretched out in different directions, until they reached the present time.

I saw that not only had Christ's cruel death rescued human beings from sin and the agony of being separated from the Father. It had also brought both Jew and Gentile together into one family, God's family here on earth.

I saw that anyone who called upon the name of the Lord Jesus Christ in repentance, whether Jew or Gentile, would now become a part of the family line of Jesus, beginning at the Cross.

I was filled with awe.

Holy Ground

After approximately ten hours in total, my vision experience began to subside late that same night.

I felt totally exhausted. My strength and my appetite had left me.

Days later the associate pastor of my previous church made an unexpected visit. This was the same man who had been present when I had been in the church building and entered my vision experience several days before.

At that moment I was lying on a mattress in my room, barely able to move any of my limbs, including even my fingers. It felt like there was a heavy weight upon my body.

The room was dark and I was contemplating everything I had seen and experienced. As I did I became aware that a heavenly presence had entered the house, and with it a sense of extraordinary serenity, calm, happiness and joy. I wasn't aware that the pastor had arrived but as he climbed the stairs to see me I sensed the presence of Christ drawing nearer and nearer to me.

To me it seemed like a brilliant and impenetrable light was approaching, emanating peace and love.

As he reached the top of the stairs and walked into my room, heaven itself seemed to arrive with him.

A powerful sensation of tranquillity began to move all over me like a gentle breeze. As it did, an intense kindness filled my heart.

Jesus and this pastor seemed to me to be one, completely indivisible.

As he sat down next to me, I was filled with joy. He took hold of my hand and as he did a wave of heavenly love and peace washed over me.

Jesus was in the room.

The pastor prayed for me briefly, uttered a few words, and then left.

But the presence of Jesus lingered.

For days afterwards I was acutely aware of His nearness to me — so much so that I was unable to connect well with the earthly realm and with normal activities. I was experiencing the sweetest communion with Jesus and it felt like I was constantly in the heavenly realms.

Not long afterwards I heard the Lord speaking to me in a grave voice.

'Remove your shoes and socks because you are standing on holy ground.'

I obeyed instantly.

I was so aware that Christ was my King and to obey Him was my all.

Not long afterwards this was reinforced when I saw Christ suspended above the earth, his nail pierced feet pointing down towards the planet. He was in complete control of the heavens and indeed the affairs of the earth, which now seemed so very small in comparison with Him.

I was suddenly so aware of the insignificance and futility of so much that happens in our world — the wars, the empire building, and the rulers who come and go.

The ascended Christ reigned above the earth with supreme authority.

Everything was under His feet.

The Family of Heaven

I went about barefoot for a few days before I felt I had permission to cover my feet again. What mattered to me was my sacred union with Christ. I didn't want anything to impair that. It was as if I had entered into a holy covenant, sealed with an unbreakable royal decree, unlike any earthly counterpart. Even marriage between a man and a woman seemed merely a shadow in comparison with the reality that I was experiencing now and the communion between the Bridegroom, Jesus, and His Bride, the church in the future. I was in a new dimension of His presence and all I desired was intimacy with Him.

So I began to delight even more in the Bible. To me it felt as if God's Word was an open channel of communication between heaven and earth.

Every time I opened it, I was struck by its immensely powerful and exhilarating effect on me. Every word was like a torrent of living water flowing through me. It was if the words had been written that very day, and especially for me.

As this sense of Christ's nearness grew, I also became aware of the great crowd of witnesses in the heavens (Hebrews 12:1). The patriarchs Moses and Joshua felt very near, as did Melchizedek and some of the twelve apostles. That isn't to say that I actually saw them or identified them by name. I was simply aware of these saints of old being present.

As I considered these saints and patriarchs I just knew that those who are alive in Christ are part of the same family as them, even though they are now in glory.

They have now gone beyond the earthly realm and are seated in the heavenly realms.

But we who are still on earth are related to them.

We are family!

My Brother Jesus

It was at this same time that I was struck by the powerful revelation that the same Jesus Christ who has all authority over the earth is also my Brother.

This of course is neither a strange nor a new doctrine. But I was overwhelmed by this thought:

The King of kings and Lord of lords, the Saviour of humanity, the beginning and the end of all things, the Creator of heaven and earth, is also my BROTHER!

We see this truth throughout the New Testament.

Jesus said, *'whoever does the will of my Father in heaven is my brother.'* (Matthew 12:50)

Then again in Hebrews 2:11 it says, *'both the one who makes men holy and those who are made holy are of the same family. So Jesus is not ashamed to call them brothers.'*

We are a part of Christ's family. We are not distant cousins once or twice removed — absolutely not! We are BROTHERS!

We cannot be much closer than that!

By becoming a human being and dwelling among us, Jesus lived like us and as such He not only suffered the same temptations known to us but was also subject to death. This meant that He was able to die as a man and thereby break the power of the one who had held mankind captive to the fear of death, the devil.

Now death had lost its sting.

Satan's grip had been shattered!

Jesus who was also fully God became a man, not only sharing in our human flesh but uniting us in family.

What a marvellous mystery!

Jesus, who was fully God, became our Brother!

Thanks to our Brother Jesus, we are now adopted into the family of God, we have become co-heirs with Him, and we inherit the promises that God gave to Abraham in the Old Testament (Ephesians 3:6).

As the Apostle Paul put it, *'if we are children, then we are heirs — heirs of God and co-heirs with Christ.'* (Romans 8:17 NIV)

The Seed of Abraham

During this time I became more and more aware of the legacy of Abraham. The Lord spoke to me about this through a symbolic representation which I later sculpted out of clay. I did not understand all of this at the time but I saw that people from all the nations of the earth have come from Abraham. Just as I had seen those long lines of people, both Jew and Gentile, filing out of David's House, so I now recognised that every human being ultimately derives from the line of Abraham.

This is a truth that Paul states in his letter to the Galatians. He says, *'if you belong to Christ, then you are Abraham's seed, and heirs according to the promise.'* (Galatians 3:29)

What Paul means is that everyone who has become a follower of Jesus Christ has also become an heir with Christ who is our Brother. This happens not by title but by spiritual union. The believer is made one with Christ Jesus.

As Jesus declared, *'I am in them and you are in me.'* (John 17:23 NIV)

Again Jesus said, *'whoever eats my flesh and drinks my blood remains in me, and I in him.'* (John 6:56 NIV)

If we are in a family union with Christ, who is our Brother, then we are also heirs of the promise given to Abraham, that in him ALL NATIONS OF THE EARTH WILL BE BLESSED.

We who are not of Jewish descent — that is, not descended from the physical family of Abraham — have now been included, or as the Scriptures declare it, we have been 'grafted in' (Romans 11). We have been made a part of the spiritual family of Abraham through Christ who is the son of David, the son of Abraham (Matthew 1:1). This makes us partakers of all the spiritual blessings promised to

Abraham's offspring.

Jesus humbled himself and became the lowest of all so that we might be lifted up and brought into complete and perfect fellowship and communion with Him — NOT AS SLAVES, NOR AS SINNERS, NOR AS DEFEATED PEOPLE, BUT WITH ALL THE RICHES THAT BELONG TO THE SON OF ABRAHAM, THE SON OF DAVID, JESUS CHRIST!

Praise God!

Ephesians 2:6 declares, 'and God raised us up with Christ and seated us with Him in heavenly realms in Christ Jesus.' (NIV)

What a marvellous mystery! Christ who is King is also our Brother. Thus through the new birth we are endowed with every spiritual blessing, privilege and authority to operate in the same way that He, our Precious Saviour Jesus Christ, operated here on earth.

The Apostle Paul declares it so wonderfully: 'and we, who with unveiled faces all reflect the Lord's glory, are being transformed into his likeness with ever-increasing glory, which comes from the Lord, who is the Spirit. For those God foreknew he also predestined to be conformed to the likeness of his Son, that he might be the firstborn among many brothers.' (2 Corinthians 3:18 NIV, Romans 8:29)

Jesus is our brother!

We are spiritually descended from David and Abraham!

We are therefore heirs to the promise!

We are the most blessed people upon the earth!

The Christ-believing Gentile and the Christ-believing Jew are together the people of God, a holy nation belonging to God.

Together we are predestined to partake of all the spiritual blessings available to us in Christ Jesus.

Praise God!

Chapter 3

Antichrist Rising

Chapter 3

Antichrist Rising

It was during this time the Lord showed me that the underground Chinese church was a critical part of His end-time strategy for world evangelisation.

He revealed that at the appointed time, during a great global upheaval and persecution, the Chinese underground church would be released, or more accurately propelled, into the world as a direct result of political pressures. Chinese Christians would preach the Gospel with unprecedented power and success in obedience to a heavenly assignment. Millions of souls would be drawn into the saving arms of Christ.

The Lord showed me that this was the reason why the Chinese church had undergone such terrible persecution. This time of trial had turned many Chinese Christians into a seasoned and well-trained army of Spirit-filled, Christ-centred saints.

These believers would be totally unwavering whenever they encounter opposition. Their persecution and troubles had become like a kind of incubator in which an abundance of fruit had been birthed. I also understood that their steadfast faithfulness under trial would be a powerful testimony to the on-looking Western church, especially since the Western church will need great encouragement not to be fearful and shrink back at the first sign of more obvious governmental persecution. I felt strongly that Brother Yun, author of the book *The Heavenly Man*, had been raised up for this purpose. He formed the first fruits, along with many others, of a much wider move of God that will be precipitated by global political unrest and an unparalleled persecution of the saints.

The Magna Carta

On another occasion during this time, on a dark evening in the winter of 1991, the Holy Spirit urgently directed me to the attic in my family home. He wanted me to retrieve a print of the Magna Carta belonging to my father.

At the time I did not know the significance of the Magna Carta or indeed what it was or why I needed to find it. All I did know was that I could sense the presence of such a spiritual darkness in England, caused specifically by spirits of paganism and witchcraft spirits.

This was not the only time I experienced this awareness of satanic darkness in the nation. Only a few days before my main vision experience I became caught up in what I can only describe as a kind of limbo between the physical and spiritual realm while I was making a journey on foot through the countryside from Wadhurst to Mayfield in Kent, England. As I walked I saw clearly that paganism, witchcraft and freemasonry had a particular stronghold in that part of the country and that the demonic spirits behind each of them were intentional about the destruction and death of the Christian family, the church, active Christians, Christian workers, Christian ministers and leaders. I saw that those who belonged to such dark and sinister groups were trying to do this through casting spells, performing occult rituals, and through secret initiation ceremonies and rites.

I also came to see that October 31st — the day on which Halloween is celebrated — was a time when witches in particular were more active than usual in this quest, and that demonic forces were in a heightened state of activity.

This should serve as a warning for any Christian that they are to play no part in the celebration of Halloween even if it masquerades as harmless fun. Ephesians 5:11 cautions us to have no fellowship with the fruitless works of darkness.

During this walk through the Kent countryside I saw and heard many things which were very disturbing to me. But probably one of the most memorable of all was the sight in the sky of a battle in the heavens.

I stopped and looked up into the cloudy sky.

To the left I could see shimmering white angels riding on pure white horses drawing bright white chariots. They were wielding white weapons, specifically swords and spears.

To the right I saw men who looked more like demons riding black horses and chariots. They bore similar weapons of medieval warfare.

The two armies charged and crashed into each other. In spite of the commotion, I couldn't hear a sound. The battle was strangely silent. The sense of looming, imminent and thick darkness was almost palpable.

It was this same presence that I was now feeling as several weeks later I clambered up into the attic to retrieve the print of the Magna Carta.

Rummaging through the many boxes in my father's attic I came across the document. It was rolled up in a plastic tube.

The Holy Spirit compelled me to take it to the garden and burn it immediately! So I took the document outdoors and set light to the corner with a match.

My father, who watched from the window, was greatly bemused by this. Why would his son do such a thing to his precious document?

British Democracy Destroyed

It was only much later, after the Lord opened my eyes to the political landscape in a revelation I received in October 2009, that I came to understand my strange actions that dark night in 1991.

What I did was prophetic. The European Union was invested with new powers that were agreed on 10th December 1991. These led to the signing of the Maastricht Treaty on 7th February 1992. These powers were eventually enshrined in law and enforced on 1st November 1993. This would destroy British democracy like paper in a fire.

The Magna Carta, Latin for 'Great Charter' or 'Great Paper', is considered by many historians to represent the beginnings of democratic government. It is because of this charter that the Queen of England is not the absolute ruler of the land. The Magna Carta paved the way for individual liberty. Originally containing 63 articles it became the cornerstone of English law and indeed all modern democracies.

The European Union is diametrically opposed to the democratic principles of the Magna Carta. With the advent of their new powers, these principles have been so weakened that they are now meaningless. In fact, they have effectively been cancelled and nullified.

By signing up to the Maastricht Treaty and the subsequent Lisbon Treaty, the United Kingdom has effectively ceded its sovereignty and is no longer governed under the constitutional law of the ideals set forth within the Magna Carta. The people of the UK are no longer truly and uniquely governed by the UK Parliament. They are now governed by the laws of the European Union and of the Brussels Parliament. These EU laws have been set up to subjugate and destroy nations by design. This destruction may be acted out in the natural realm but it is actually a spiritual act of wickedness in high places. The prime movers behind this wickedness were those occult forces whose dark presence I had sensed when I was climbing up to the attic to retrieve the Magna Carta — paganism, witchcraft and Freemasonry.

The Antichrist

During this time I saw the Antichrist standing in the heavenly realms wearing a black robe adorned with golden buttons. White fur surrounded the hem, collar and the cuffs. On his head he wore a kingly, jewel-encrusted, golden crown and in his hand he held a golden sceptre.

I saw another figure, a woman also adorned in black, with long straight and shiny blond hair. She was wearing a garment similar to the Antichrist.

As I looked at her I saw that she had a seductive and proud spirit, a spirit like Jezebel in the Old Testament. She also had a crown upon her head, and as I looked, although I did not understand this, I understood that she was a demonic counterfeit of the Holy Spirit.

These two demonic beings stood shoulder to shoulder on what looked like a gigantic chess board. They were strategically positioned, as if they were waiting to make their move to enter into the world together at the appointed time.

I then saw Jesus Christ dressed in similar attire. However, his robe was blood red — the collar, cuffs and hem made of the purest of white fur. He too held a golden sceptre. It was tipped with a golden orb about four inches in diameter and encrusted with precious stones.

Upon His head He wore a golden crown. This was also bejewelled with precious stones. It was the crown of the King of kings and the Lord of lords.

Standing next to Christ, shoulder to shoulder, was the person of the Holy Spirit.

They too stood waiting to enter the world at the appointed moment in the end-times of history.

The Imminent Return of Christ

During this whole time I was acutely aware of the nearness of the second coming of the Lord Jesus and that we were in the closing stages of history. The tangible presence of His coming charged the atmosphere around me. Yet I was troubled in my spirit to know when exactly the end of all things would occur. But I could not find out. It is worth noting here that the Scriptures counsel us that it is not possible to know the exact day and hour of the return of Christ (Matthew 24:36). If anyone then comes and announces precise dates we can be sure that this person is in error or, worse still, intent on deceiving the brethren.

It was at this time that the Lord showed me specific people in the church that were considered by other Christians to be the least in the Kingdom of God.

These saints were unjustly judged and looked down on when in reality they were to be greatly honoured. The Lord considered them to be the greatest in the Kingdom! These Christians were silently but faithfully fulfilling their end-time callings.

I eagerly made a point of meeting with these Christians, wondering if they might be able to help me understand the time of the end.

A Deceptive Ruler

Throughout this time the wonder and mystery of the virgin birth occupied my thoughts although I did not receive a vision of this blessed truth.

I also had a strong perception, but again it was not a vision, that a ruler was rising and deception would mark his reign and that He would claim that he had been conceived in a similar or in the same fashion as our Glorious Saviour Jesus Christ.

I do not know if this meant that he would claim to be born of a virgin or not. All I knew was that his origins would be shrouded in mystery and his claims — whatever they might be — would be complete falsehood and from a satanic source.

These thoughts grieved my spirit greatly. It caused me much pain that a man could posture in such a blasphemous manner, deceiving the masses in the near future.

Food Offered to Idols

It was also at this time that I sat around the table with my family to eat. As I put a piece of meat in my mouth I instantly heard the Holy Spirit speak in what felt like an audible way in my right ear.

'Do not eat food that has been offered up to idols.'

I immediately felt nauseous. It seemed to me as if the meat was off. I could no longer eat it.

I already knew that the New Testament did not place this kind of restriction on a believer so I did not understand why I'd been told this. Only later did it become clear that this incident was supposed to be a prophetic warning. The Lord was alerting me to the fact that the meat had been offered up to idols.

How could that be?

Today it is becoming more and more common in the West for animals to be slaughtered in the ritualistic manner of Islam. This kind of practice is known as 'halal.' The animal is killed while the butcher faces Mecca and recites that 'Allah is the greatest.'

Looking back I now understand that the phrase 'meat being offered to idols' was a warning about the growing influence that Islam was going to have on Western society in the future, even down to the mundane issues of eating.

This struck me as very much more than a minor caution about diet. The Lord showed me very clearly that Islam would feature significantly in the events leading up to the second coming of Christ.

The Bottomless Pit

On another occasion I experienced what I can only describe as what the Scriptures call 'the bottomless pit', or 'the abyss', from which the Bible says the Antichrist will rise during earth's final years.

I had been unable to sleep all night long because of the continuous visions passing through my mind. Finally I fell asleep and straight away it felt as if my spirit somehow left my body. This seemed so real to me that I was convinced it actually happened.

The moment I fell asleep I experienced my spirit abruptly leaving my body and hurtling down into a dark chasm. The sensation of falling was as real to me as any waking experience.

I fell at an incredible speed, faster and faster, thousands and thousands of feet down into the darkness of the pit.

Down and down I went.

As I fell, I became aware that this pit had no end and I knew that I would continue to fall for eternity.

The width of the pit was enormous and the darkness was incalculably deep. It appeared to be about one mile in diameter but it might have been narrower — it was difficult to estimate.

The walls of the chasm appeared to be made of some kind of dense black matter that was impenetrable and quite unlike any solid material found on the earth. It was more like lifeless, compacted dark matter. There was energy in it and yet it seemed dead.

Nothing could escape from this hole and nothing could enter into it, except through the opening through which I'd passed.

It was a terrifying place; the atmosphere was tinged with evil. Although I did not feel the presence of any other living beings with me as I fell, I was concerned that there was something lurking much further into the chasm.

What was deeply disturbing to me as I continued to fall was the growing realisation that in this place a person was completely and utterly separated from the living God. It was as though God did not exist in that pit. I couldn't find His presence anywhere. Indeed nothing seemed to exist here. There was no trace of God's creation at all.

As I looked out into this black void I was aware that on the other side of it the entire created universe existed, teaming with millions upon millions of stars, where God sat enthroned in the heavens.

But it was impossible to reach it.

As the fearful awareness of my predicament grew I frantically twisted myself as I fell through the dense darkness, trying to look above me to the place where I had originally entered. This was now thousands of miles above and beyond me. I stretched out my arm in desperation as though to grasp onto something but my hands just snatched at empty space and I continued to fall.

It was then that I made out a pinprick of light in the far distance above me. I hadn't noticed it before. It was as though the pit had somehow been opened as a response to my reaching out for help.

Then with my arm outstretched, I reached with my hand towards the speck of light. At this point I became aware of what I can only describe as a large angel standing at the top of the entrance.

The angel appeared to either sweep down the left side of the opening, or to use its power from where it had been watching me plummet, to pull me up at an immense speed until I exited out of the pit.

At that moment it felt as if my spirit instantly rejoined my body with a jolt, and I found myself jumping up from the bed and standing upright.

I was completely startled.

'I just died!' I cried.

I do not know if I had literally died but the sensation of dying and leaving my body was real enough to me.

Within minutes I knew by revelation that the source of the writings and the beliefs behind the occult, new age, religious sects and false religions came directly from the spirit that dwells in this bottomless pit.

Many of these doctrines, as I realised in that moment, had been dictated supernaturally via automatic writing by fallen angels.

All these false religious ideas are Antichrist doctrines because they defiantly refuse to acknowledge that Jesus is the Christ. It should come as little surprise then that these doctrines come from such a God forsaken place.

It is out of this place that the Antichrist will ascend in the last days and wreak havoc upon the earth, along with his henchman, the False Prophet, who will propagate a deceptive religious ideology.

The Bible tells us that in the latter days some will abandon the faith and follow after false doctrines. This time is known as the great apostasy. The ideas promulgated in these teachings will come from deceiving spirits and things taught by demons. As 1 Timothy 4:1 says: '*now the Spirit expressly says that in latter times some will depart from the faith, giving heed to deceiving spirits and doctrines of demons*' (NKJV).

In visions of the Apostle John, recorded in the Book of Revelation, John saw the Antichrist (or the beast) rising from this bottomless pit during the end times.

'*When they [the two witnesses] finish their testimony, the beast that ascends out of the bottomless pit will make war against them, overcome them, and kill them.'* (Revelation 11:7 NKJV) *'The beast that you saw was, and is not, and will ascend out of the bottomless pit and go to perdition.'* (Revelation 17:8 NKJV)

The bottomless pit also features in other significant end-time events. It is the place that the Bible says will be opened at the sound of the fifth trumpet blast. When this occurs, a multitude of demons — fallen angels in the form of mutated locusts — will rise from its smoke and attack people and sting them for five months. All those who have not received the seal of God upon their foreheads will suffer terrible pain and death.

These demon locusts have a king over them described as the angel of the bottomless pit, whose name in the Hebrew tongue is *Abaddon*, in Greek *Apollyon*, which means the *Destroyer* (Revelation 9:1-12).

The Antichrist will likely be possessed by this demon or will be heavily influenced and draw great power from it.

The bottomless pit literally means 'the shaft of the abyss.' It is a prison for demons. It is also the place where Satan will be bound for 1000 years after the battle of Armageddon.

Revelation 20:1-3 reads: *'then I saw an angel coming down from heaven, having the key to the bottomless pit and a great chain in his hand. He laid hold of the dragon, that serpent of old, who is the Devil and Satan, and bound him for a thousand years; and he cast him into the bottomless pit...'*

A Vision of Hell

Finally I saw a portion of hell.

This vision came to me in a sudden flash and totally without warning. I was not expecting it and neither was I considering such things when it came upon me. It appeared rather like a lightning storm at night when the sky is lit up and the trees and buildings can be briefly seen before the lightning vanishes and the darkness suddenly returns.

Although the vision must have lasted no longer than a second I saw enough to give a detailed description of what I saw.

I saw countless people waiting to be damned forever because they chose to ignore the message of the Good News found only in Christ Jesus our Lord. They were lined up in queues upon an elevated walkway on a craggy mountain pass, silently waiting to enter a city of eternal damnation.

They appeared not to be speaking. Their mouths were closed. This I considered strange given the vast volume of people and their close proximity to one another.

Fire consumed that city with a ferocious heat and many of the gutted buildings glowed orange as they disintegrated before my very eyes.

Remember that the Biblical references to hell being a place of fire are numerous. Jesus himself made many references to hell being a place of fire: Matthew 5:22; 13:42; 13:50; 18:8; 18:9; 25:41; Mark 9:43; 9:44; 9:45; 9:46; 9:47; 9:48; Luke 16:24.

Hell is an awful reality.

Thus it was that I cried out in a great urgency of soul. The pain of seeing all this seared my heart so deeply that I staggered and almost physically collapsed at the sheer horror of it. As the vision vanished I panicked for the lost.

I then pleaded with a person who had not yet departed this life but who professed to be a Christian. But this person was just a religious churchgoer and had no living relationship with our Lord at all. To my utter bewilderment and disbelief this person was impassive to my anguished pleas to know Christ and receive eternal salvation before it was too late. They were simply too proud to care and therefore unable to see the truth.

Coming Back to Earth

Months later I eventually reconnected completely with the earthly realm and the revelations ceased altogether.

Such was the void left by leaving the spiritual realm and also the trauma caused by the many things that I had experienced and witnessed that it became incredibly difficult for me to adjust to normal life.

At the time I did not understand everything about the vision experiences. I didn't understand why they had happened or what their purpose was. These questions played upon my mind for many years to come.

I did not discuss these things with anyone because it was too disturbing to talk about and too difficult for me to comprehend.

The experience profoundly affected my life. Every vivid memory and each exacting detail weighed heavily upon me for many years.

In fact, it would be nineteen years later, in October 2009, I would begin to understand the full meaning and import of what I had seen back in October 1991. In October 2009 I experienced a dream vision in which the Lord warned me of the dangers of further integration with the European Union. Then my eyes were opened to the political and eschatological climate of the day, and I came to fully understand the interpretation of the entire ten hour vision experience and subsequent experiences.

The details of the 2009 dream and their interpretation and application can be found in my book, *Trumpet Blast Warning*.

Just as the dream vision came in October of 2009 and at a key moment for Europe, so too did the vision of October 1991.

The Maastricht Treaty, the Treaty on European Union, was drafted the following month.

The importance of the Maastricht Treaty cannot be

underestimated. Wide and sweeping changes were implemented through it. The Treaty significantly advanced the European agenda for deeper and further integration. A further loss of national sovereignty of the participating nations took place and a giant leap forward was taken in the goal to create a European super state. The Treaty would formally establish the European Union and it would pave the way for the single Euro currency. This Euro currency was the fledgling idea for a global currency, thereby moving the world one step closer to what we are warned about in Biblical prophecy — a one world monetary system.

In 1992 the then German Chancellor, Helmut Kohl, testified to the magnitude of the Maastricht Treaty when he said:

'In Maastricht we laid the foundation stone for the completion of the European Union. The European Union Treaty introduces a new and decisive stage in the process of European Union which within a few years will lead to the creation of what the founding fathers of modern Europe dreamed of after the last war; the United States of Europe.'[1]

These are signs of the times.

They are in fact signs of the end-times.

1. Cris Shaw, *Building Europe, The Cultural Politics of European Integration*, (Routledge, 2000), 211

Part II

The Interpretation

Chapter 4

He Who Has An Ear

Chapter 4

He Who Has an Ear

In the first part of this chapter we will look at the importance of interpreting visions and dreams. In the second part we will look at how visions, dreams and their interpretation flow out of intimacy with God. We will also look at the relationship between intimacy with God and the symbolic language He often uses to communicate with us.

The importance of Interpretation

Whenever the Lord gives a vision or a dream to His people, this needs to be subjected to a process of interpretation. Just as the Holy Spirit inspires the revelation, so the Holy Spirit inspires the interpretation.

We can see this so clearly in the life of the Old Testament prophet called Daniel. Daniel was one of about 50,000 Jews sent into exile by Nebuchadnezzar, the king of Babylon. As an exile in Babylon, Daniel was given the opportunity to serve the king in the royal court. Daniel's trustworthiness as a man gave him proximity to the king. This was no accident. God had given Daniel a supernatural gift of wisdom to interpret peoples' dreams.

And the king was starting to have some very strange dreams.

At the start of Daniel chapter 2, we read that the king is having some interrupted nights. He is becoming more and more restless because of his unsettling dreams. Feeling troubled, the king sends for his court magicians, sorcerers and astrologers and asks them (a) to tell him what he has dreamed and (b) to tell him what the dream means.

None of his advisors can help. They have no idea what the king has dreamed. They don't have the supernatural ability to see what another man has dreamed.

It is then that the young Daniel finds his way into the king's presence. He asks the king for time to ask the Lord both the nature and the meaning of the king's dream. The king grants the boy's request.

Daniel goes back to his friends and they pray. That night the Lord gives Daniel the details and the interpretation of the king's dream. Daniel's response is to praise God for giving him wisdom and discernment:

> *"Praise be to the name of God forever and ever;*
> *wisdom and power are his.*
> *He changes times and seasons;*
> *he deposes kings and raises up others.*
> *He gives wisdom to the wise*
> *and knowledge to the discerning.*
> *He reveals deep and hidden things;*
> *he knows what lies in darkness,*
> *and light dwells with him.*
> *I thank and praise you, God of my ancestors:*
> *you have given me wisdom and power,*
> *you have made known to me what we asked of you,*
> *you have made known to us the dream of the king."*
> (Daniel 2:22-23 NIV)

The next day the prophet Daniel goes back to the king and tells him the content of the dream. The king had seen in his dream a great statue, with its head made of gold, chest and arms of silver, belly and thighs of bronze, legs of iron and feet of both iron and clay. In the dream the king saw a great rock — not cut by human hands — strike the legs and feet of the statue, causing the whole edifice to be pulverised, its remaining particles swept away by the wind. Daniel tells the king that this represents kingdoms that will rise and fall in the future. The rock represents a kingdom that cannot be shaken or destroyed — a kingdom belonging to God, a kingdom that will outlast all the other kingdoms and surpass them all.

The king's reaction is instant. He is struck with awe that the young Jewish man in his court knows what he has dreamed. He is startled and convinced by the interpretation which this young Jewish exile has given. His response is immediate and profound:

Then King Nebuchadnezzar fell prostrate before Daniel and paid him honour and ordered that an offering and incense be presented to him. The king said to Daniel, "Surely your God is the God of gods and the Lord of kings and a revealer of mysteries, for you were able to reveal this mystery."

What a miraculous transformation? This king who has sanctioned occult practices and worshipped false pagan gods acknowledges that Daniel's God is the one, true, living God of the universe!

In short, he turns momentarily away from the darkness and reverences the light.

Such is the power of revelation when it is subjected to interpretation!

Prophecy as Foretelling

This is all very relevant to *Beyond Earthly Realms* because I believe my visions were prophecies concerning the future, as was the case with the dreams given to the king.

Prophecy often falls into two categories. There is first of all

forth-telling. Forth-telling is usually a prophet's declaration of something past or present. It doesn't have a predictive element. It is simply the prophet announcing the thoughts of God — or, as we would say in the New Covenant era, 'the mind of Christ' — to a person, to people, to a nation. This doesn't have a future tense to it. It is a revelatory insight into either the way things have been or the way things are.

The second kind of prophecy does however have a future tense. This is **foretelling**. In this kind of prophecy the prophet hears or sees something with the help of the Holy Spirit, something that has a bearing on the future. In this kind of prophecy the prophet sees what is going to happen or what God intends to do. This can either inspire repentance, causing future judgment to be averted, or it can inspire hope, causing God's future blessing to be embraced. Either way, this kind of prophecy has the character of foretelling.

King Nebuchadnezzar was used to his occult advisors engaging in fortune telling. This was not a trustworthy art. The practices involved in them were demonic in nature and demons, indeed the devil too, will not accurately predict details of the future. Occult sources are most unreliable as they are inspired by the devil, who is a *hater of the truth* and *the father of lies* (John 8:44 NLT). It is therefore only the prophetic gift, inspired by the Spirit of God, *who cannot lie* (Titus 1:2), which offers a true vision of what is to come.

This is the point that Daniel makes in verse 29 of chapter 2. He says to Nebuchadnezzar,

"As Your Majesty was lying there, your mind turned to things to come, and the revealer of mysteries showed you what is going to happen."

Notice that phrase, "what is going to happen." Daniel knew that he had been given prophetic revelation about what was to come in the future.

But he was not a fortune teller. He was a foreteller.

He wasn't a psychic. He was a prophet.

He wasn't making things up. He was giving future facts.

He wasn't using his gift to promote himself. He was using it to give glory to God.

In these and in many other ways Daniel operated in a totally different spirit from those around him. And as a result he accurately foretold the future.

Future History Revealed

Daniel served God six hundred years before Christ came and inaugurated the Kingdom of God on the earth. Before that time, various Empires rose and fell, just as Daniel had predicted they would.

The first Empire was that of Nebuchadnezzar — the Babylonian Empire. This was symbolized by the head made of gold.

The second Empire was the Medo-Persian Empire, represented by the silver.

The third was the Empire of the Greeks, symbolized by the bronze.

The fourth was the Roman Empire, symbolized by the iron, and the feet of iron and clay symbolized a resurgence of the Roman Empire in these last days.[1]

All these Empires rose and fell in the centuries after Daniel (indeed, centuries later a revived 'Roman' Empire would establish itself in Europe and spread throughout the earth). When the Roman Empire had been established, a Rock appeared just as Daniel prophesied.

This was the Rock of Ages — Jesus Christ, born in the time of the reign of Caesar Augustus.

This Rock represented a kingdom that would never fall, never die, and never fly away on the wind. This Kingdom is the Kingdom of God, the Kingdom of Heaven here on earth.

Since the time of Christ's baptism onwards, this Kingdom has been spreading across the earth. One day, when Christ the King of kings returns, this kingdom will be fully established. It will crush the final empire – the revived 'Roman' empire — and there will be new heavens and a new earth in which God will reign forever and ever, Amen!

See then how Daniel's interpretation of the king's dream contains accurate predictions about the development of future history and the acts of God in the rise and fall of human kingdoms. While beyond *Beyond Earthly Realms* touches on forth-telling, its overarching character is foretelling — with a focus on future global history.

I believe that within the visions and their interpretation in *Beyond Earthly Realms* God has revealed 'what is going to happen.'

Interpreting these Visions

This brings me back to the importance of interpretation. The truth is God sometimes speaks in a mysterious way. He doesn't always give the kind of words that we see for example in the Book of Haggai, where the Holy Spirit simply says through his prophet, 'The Lord is with you.' This kind of prophecy requires very little interpretation. However, Haggai's contemporary, the prophet Zechariah, is a very different matter. His dreams and visions are full of very strange symbolism. Where Haggai is very prosaic, Zechariah is very poetic.

This shows that God sometimes says things through enigmatic symbolism. One of the reasons for this is that it draws us into intimate fellowship with Him, as we seek to interpret what He is saying.

When Jesus walked the earth he often communicated the secrets of the Kingdom in symbolism too. In Matthew 13 we read, *"The knowledge of the secrets of heaven has been given to you, but not to them. This is why I speak to them in parables, though seeing, they do not see; though hearing, they do not hear or understand."* (Matthew 13:11,13)

Only those who were hungering and thirsting for righteousness would have the right kind of heart to receive and interpret the symbolic message hidden within the parable. For those whose hearts were closed to Jesus — for example, many of the religious leaders of the day — His message was meaningless. They were unable to interpret what He said because they didn't have the Spirit of God in them. 1 Corinthians 2:14 explains this: *"But the natural man does not receive the things of the Spirit of God, for they are foolishness to him; nor can he know them, because they are spiritually discerned."*

Jesus also spoke this way because he didn't want to 'cast what was sacred before the unholy' — or, in another translation, 'cast pearls before swine' (Matthew 7:6). In other words, Jesus did not want to share what was precious with those who would only reject or ridicule what He was saying. Jesus also warned that sharing holy things with those who do not receive them can lead to persecution (Matthew 7:6). And so, depending on the occasion, Jesus would preach in metaphors and during those times it was up to His followers to search God's heart for the answer.

That is not to say the religious people of Jesus' day did not have the opportunity to open their hearts. The Pharisee Nicodemus was one such religious man who did open his heart and believe (John 3:1-21). Today everyone has the opportunity to hear the message of the Kingdom and understand it. However, a hard heart will always stand in the way, dulling our perception and deafening our ears. Remember that it was Pharaoh's hard heart that prevented him from hearing the word of the Lord. This attitude of heart not only stopped up his spiritual ears, but it also produced in him such a violent rage that he pursued Moses with vengeance. It is of course this spirit that murdered the prophets.

It is this spirit that murdered the Son of God, Christ Jesus.

So then, this should be a warning to us, that we ourselves do not quench the Spirit of God. Let us not despise bible prophecy. But rather let us with all diligence search the scriptures in order to understand what God is saying. Let us also value prophetic gifts in this present day, seeing that they do have a place in the church, and importantly testing everything, holding fast to what is good. Let us not use our testing though as an occasion to scoff at such gifts (1 Thessalonians 5:20).

Let us not harden our hearts as Israel did in the wilderness, though they had seen many miraculous signs (Psalm 95:8-9). But let us hear His voice calling out to come to Him today (Psalm 95:7)! The consequences of a deaf ear are disturbing. We are told in Psalm 95:11 that those who do not listen will never enter the Promised Land, the place of rest that God planned for us.

This is why Jesus is always asking us to open our spiritual ears to His Word. He says, "If anyone hears my voice", or in another place, "He who has an ear let him hear what the Spirit is saying", or again, "Listen to what I say and try to understand" (Matthew 15:10). If we don't listen to Jesus, we will be left out in the dark, never to enter the rest that He promised for us long ago.

Having Ears to Hear

By concealing the secrets of the Kingdom in this way those who desire to hear and understand must come away from the noise of the world and draw near to Jesus. Only in this place can we hear and interpret what He is saying. Earthly noise muffles the sound of His voice.

A good example of this is a story in the life of Elijah the prophet, found in 1 Kings 19. Elijah was on the run from Queen Jezebel. Her vengeance towards Elijah had caused him to run away in despair.

Interestingly a false prophetic declaration by Jezebel over Elijah, in which she said he would be dead by the next night, took root in him. So much so that Elijah actually began to pray the very thing that she had decreed over him! In Elijah's despair he prayed that he would die!

There are many voices competing in us and outside of us to have pre-eminence over what God is saying to us. Fears, worry, anxieties, worldly desires, or just like Elijah experienced, a spirit can haunt us to the point of such discouragement that we hope to die. These voices can cry so loudly that we become totally inept at hearing God's voice.

In the story of Elijah it is interesting what happened next.

Firstly God did not heed the prayer of Elijah but rather sent an angel to wake him up out of his sleep of discouragement, and to encourage him and to feed him, and to send him on a forty day journey.

Elijah eventually arrived at the mountain of God, where he stayed in a cave.

Now that God had Elijah's attention, He asked him a simple question, "Why are you here Elijah?"

Elijah explained to God that Jezebel was out to kill him. God then did something very interesting. He asked Elijah to go out of the mountain cave and to stand before Him. As he did, the Lord passed by as a mighty windstorm hit the mountain. It was such a terrible blast that the rocks were torn loose. Yet we are told THE LORD WAS NOT IN THE WIND. After the wind, the Lord passed by again and an earthquake struck. Yet we are told THE LORD WAS NOT IN THE EARTHQUAKE. After the earthquake, the Lord passed by again, this time during a fire. Yet we are told THE LORD WAS NOT IN THE FIRE!

The Lord then repeated his question to Elijah, "What are you doing here?"

What was the Lord teaching Elijah through this?

I believe one of the lessons was, that even when the Lord is present, it can sometimes be impossible to hear Him over competing noises.

I wonder if those three acts of nature were somehow symbolic of Elijah's present circumstances? Did the wind represent his running away? Did the earthquake represent his fear of sudden death? Did the fire represent the anxieties of his heart?

After all the turmoil that unfolded before Elijah — the wind, the earthquake and the fire — we are told that Elijah eventually heard the Lord in 'a still small voice'. You see Elijah had to tune his heart to God's heart. He had to turn his ear towards heaven and listen carefully. Elijah had to draw close to God again. He had to lay everything aside and come into God's presence in order to hear His voice and interpret what He was saying.

Intimacy and Prophecy

Dreams, visions, revelations and interpretations are born out of intimacy with God. These gifts are simply God speaking with us, whereby He shows us what is on His heart; they are nothing more and nothing less. Isn't it an awesome privilege that the God of heaven wishes to share His heart with us?

All we need do is ready ourselves continually before Him, and call out to Him with all sincerity and urgency of heart, and He will answer, and He will tell us so many things.

If you find that hard to believe, look at Jeremiah 33:3, *"Call to Me and I will answer you and tell you great and incomprehensible things you do not know."* (HCSB) Look at Revelation 4:1-2: *"And the first voice which I heard was like a trumpet speaking with me, saying, Come up here, and I will show you things which must take place after this. Immediately I was in the Spirit; and behold, a throne set in heaven, and One sat on the throne."* (NKJV)

Notice that in Jeremiah 33:3 incomprehensible mysteries are understood simply through a conversation with the Lord. When we give attention to the Father, He gives attention to us. In the context of such intimate communion He will always answer. Through conversation, God will share with us His mysteries, or things yet to come.

Notice also how the Apostle John hears a voice like a trumpet saying, "come up here, and I will show you…" Immediately we are told that John is transported into the very throne room of God! John must first come up close into the very heart of where God is — up close and into intimate fellowship with Him. It is in this place where He is shown, mysteries, or, in this instance, secrets of future events. This happened to Moses too. When God gave Moses the Ten Commandments, it was not in a distant or terrifying way. No, it was simply through an intimate encounter. Moses and God, we are told in scripture, conversed with each other just like friends (Exodus 33:11). Imagine that! This friendship is not only reserved for the likes of Moses though. It is reserved for you and for me!

Daniel too, knew this intimacy. As he saw disturbing mysteries and interpreted the future rise and fall of empires, he was reminded by the angel that he was greatly beloved of the Lord (Daniel 10:10). Revelation and relationship go hand in hand. On a side note, just as Daniel received strange visions, we should recognise that God does not always wish to share pleasant matters with us. Sometimes God can share alarming things, just as He did through His messengers in the bible. We should also recognise that visionary experiences can occur with such momentum that the resulting effect upon the recipient can be quite negative.

For example the Apostle John was so disturbed by all that God had shown him concerning the end times, he became sick to the stomach (Revelation 10:10). We are also told that after Daniel received his visions he became worn out, and lay exhausted for several days (Daniel 8:27). We are also told that his strength left, his face turned deathly pale, he was overcome with anguish, and he could hardly breathe (Daniel 10:8; 10:16-17).

Nevertheless, whether God shows us beautiful mysteries, shares His broken heart, or reveals terrible and disturbing future events, we can consider it such a wonderful privilege and mystery that He would choose to speak with us as a friend to a friend.

We can see then that intimacy with God, through His Son Jesus Christ, is a prerequisite for interpreting the mysteries of God. Without friendship with God, it is impossible.

Drawing Closer to Jesus

In conclusion what does all this tell us?

In order to hear and interpret what God is saying, we must have our ears turned towards Him. We must be in close union with Him, and with the cry of Jesus, hear what the Spirit is saying to us.

"He who has an ear, let him hear..." (Revelation 2:7)

Here then we see the importance of having a second part to *Beyond Earthly Realms*, a part devoted to the interpretation of my visions.

Since my main vision had eight sequential sections, we will look at each of these in turn over the next few chapters. These are:

1. A Trumpet Blast

2. The Dark Rock

3. The Tower of Gold

4. The Spirit-Filled Saints

5. After the Rapture

6. The Blessed Trinity

7. The Cross of Calvary

8. The Roman Spear, House of David and the Family of Christ.

Friends, as you read the interpretation of the vision in the following chapters, it is my prayer that you will draw ever closer to Jesus in fellowship with Him, and as you do He will share more of His heart with you.

1. Jason Carter, *Trumpet Blast Warning*, (Trumpet Blast Publishing, 2014), 97

Chapter 5

The Trumpet Blast

Chapter 5

The Trumpet Blast

My vision experience began when I was taken to a place where I found myself standing among the stars of heaven. Immediately I was greeted by a long, continuous blast of a trumpet.

Here's the description:

I was now taken beyond the earthly, physical realm into an altogether different reality.

I saw the heavens opened before me and I found myself standing in the air, as though suspended with no ground beneath me.

There I stood in the deep blue space amongst the stars of the heavens looking out into eternity.

As I remained suspended in the air, I heard the deafening and continuous noise of what sounded like the blast of a trumpet. It could be heard all around.

Why did my vision sequence begin with this trumpet blast?

When we look at the Scriptures there are references to trumpets everywhere. We tend to think of brass instruments when we read the word 'trumpet.' But in the Bible the word often refers to the ram's horn, known in Hebrew as the shofar. This sound is utterly unique. Indeed, it has a quite haunting, other-worldly pitch, as if bringing the resonant frequencies of heaven to earth.

The shofar is mentioned 72 times in the Old Testament. While it is used for a number of different purposes, it was often blown as a warning.

We see this in Ezekiel 33:3-6 where the loud and unmistakable sound of the shofar is used to warn God's people of imminent danger:

The word of the Lord came to me: 'Son of man, speak to your people and say to them: "When I bring the sword against a land, and the people of the land choose one of their men and make him their watchman, and he sees the sword coming against the land and blows the trumpet to warn the people, then if anyone hears the trumpet but does not heed the warning and the sword comes and takes their life, their blood will be on their own head. Since they heard the sound of the trumpet but did not heed the warning, their blood will be on their own head. If they had heeded the warning, they would have saved themselves. But if the watchman sees the sword coming and does not blow the trumpet to warn the people and the sword comes and takes someone's life, that person's life will be taken because of their sin, but I will hold the watchman accountable for their blood."'

Here the connotation of the sound of the shofar is unmistakable. The watchman on the walls has the responsibility to awaken God's people and to alert them to the imminent approach of God's judgment. The watchman is a metaphor for the prophet who keeps a vigil on the walls, looking out for the sword of the Lord coming against the land, sounding the shofar when he sees it approaching. Those who hear and respond will be saved. To those who ignore the warning, God says 'your blood will be on your own heads.'

In the Book of Joel (2:1-2), the trumpet blast is used to warn

God's people that the Day of the Lord is imminent:

> *Blow the trumpet in Zion;*
> *sound the alarm on my holy hill.*
> *Let all who live in the land tremble,*
> *for the day of the Lord is coming.*
> *It is close at hand —*
> *a day of darkness and gloom,*
> *a day of clouds and blackness.*
> *Like dawn spreading across the mountains*
> *a large and mighty army comes,*
> *such as never was in ancient times*
> *nor ever will be in ages to come.*

In the New Testament, the Day of the Lord is associated with the Second Coming of Jesus Christ at the climax of history.

This event will be signalled by a loud blast of a heavenly trumpet — a sound that will quite literally be loud enough to wake the dead.

So for example the Apostle Paul writes that the trumpet blast of God will herald the second coming of Christ (1 Thessalonians 4:16 NKJV):

For the Lord Himself will descend from heaven with a shout, with the voice of an archangel, and with the trumpet of God. And the dead in Christ will rise first.

In the Book of Revelation chapters 8-11, the Apostle John hears seven trumpet blasts, all of which herald apocalyptic, end-time events on the earth. These seven trumpets are in the hands of seven angels before the throne of God.

After the first angel blew the first trumpet hail and fire mingled with blood was thrown upon the earth and a third of the trees and all green grass was burned up.

The second trumpet was then sounded and something like a great burning mountain was cast into the sea and a third of the sea became blood, killing a third of all sea creatures and destroying a third of all ships.

As the third trumpet sounded a great burning and poisonous star fell from heaven and hit the fresh water rivers polluting a third of them. Many people died from drinking the contaminated water.

Then the fourth angel blew the fourth trumpet after which a third of the sun, moon and stars were darkened. This angel cried out in great distress to the inhabitants of the earth because of the remaining three trumpet blasts.

The fifth trumpet blast heralded a star falling from heaven to earth. This 'star' was given access to open the bottomless pit. On opening it, so much smoke arose that it darkened the sky and polluted the air. Then out of its smoke arose mutated locusts that stung all those people who were not marked by God.

Then the sixth angel blew their trumpet and this released four angels who had been prepared to kill a third of humanity and a vast army numbering two hundred million arose which released plagues upon the people. The purpose of this was to give the people an opportunity to repent of their wicked ways so that God could save them, just as he did in the story of Moses and Pharaoh. Tragically, as with Pharaoh, the people hardened their hearts.

Finally the seventh trumpet blast sounded and loud voices in heaven cried out saying, *'the kingdoms of this world are become the kingdoms of our Lord, and of his Christ; and he shall reign forever and ever'* (Revelation 11:15 NKJV). The Temple of God was then opened and the Ark of His Covenant was seen and there came lightning, thunder, an earthquake and great hail.

It is interesting that my vision sequence began with a loud and continuous blast of a heavenly shofar. Clearly the sound was intended to alert me, and indeed you who are reading this, to the things that are to come.

When the Apostle John had his sequence of visions — visions

which he recorded for us in the Book of Revelation — these started with the sound of a shofar. *'I was in the Spirit on the Lord's Day, and I heard behind me a loud voice, as of a trumpet.'* (Revelation 1:10 NKJV) *'And the first voice which I heard was like a trumpet speaking with me, saying, "Come up here, and I will show you things which must take place after this"'* (Revelation 4:1 NKJV).

While I do not want to compare myself with the Apostle John, I do believe it's no coincidence that my vision experience began with a trumpet blast.

This set the tone for the whole vision experience.

It sounded an unforgettable note of warning.

Chapter 6

Encroaching Darkness

Chapter 6

Encroaching Darkness

As the trumpet blast continued I saw what looked like a dark rock hurtling towards the earth.

I looked upwards and saw something that resembled a gigantic dark rock — like a vast boulder — hurtling with incredible speed towards the earth. The rock looked like a star falling from the heavens. Its essence was utterly evil. The rock hit the earth with a sudden and devastating impact.

The earth shuddered and responded as though in terrible agony. The place where the rock had landed was Europe. I let out a piercing and terrible cry of pain. Somehow I knew in my spirit that something demonic had come to Europe and I felt the searing pain of the impact myself.

The symbol of the Rock is often used in Scripture.

Sometimes this symbol is positive, having a connotation of goodness and light. So, for example, the rock that I mentioned in chapter 4 was most definitely from the kingdom of light not the kingdom of darkness. The statue made of gold, silver, bronze, iron and clay was struck by a rock not made by human hands, destroying the statue completely, scattering its minute pulverised pieces to the four winds.

Here the Rock is clearly 'the Rock of Ages,' Jesus Christ. God sends his Son from heaven at the time of the iron empire (the time of the Romans) and Christ's kingdom causes all the world systems that oppose God to come crashing down.

Hallelujah!

But the image of the rock in my vision sequence was quite different from this. It was most certainly not a positive symbol. It wasn't a symbol of Jesus and it did not come from the kingdom of light. It was emphatically a dark rock — a rock that fell from the heavens like a star.

Here it's really important to emphasize the word 'star'. This Rock was a stellar rock.

In the Bible, the image of a falling star is inextricably linked with Satan, whose name means 'Adversary'.

Satan wasn't originally called 'Satan.' He was originally called 'Lucifer', which means 'Morning star' — a beautiful name for one who was at first a beautiful angel. When he fell from heaven Satan lost his right to be called the 'Star of the Morning' and plummeted like a shooting star from heaven to earth. He then became a dark angel.

There is a description of this in Isaiah 14:12-15, a passage that has a two-level meaning. Level 1 refers to the demise of a king of Babylon in the era of the prophet Isaiah. Level 2 refers to the demise of Satan, who fell from heaven after he rebelled against God out of pride and jealousy:

How you have fallen from heaven,
morning star, son of the dawn!
You have been cast down to the earth,
you who once laid low the nations!

You said in your heart,
'I will ascend to the heavens;
I will raise my throne
above the stars of God;
I will sit enthroned on the mount of assembly,
on the utmost heights of Mount Zaphon.
I will ascend above the tops of the clouds;
I will make myself like the Most High.'
But you are brought down to the realm of the dead,
to the depths of the pit.

Jesus clearly saw this tragic fall before the creation of man. He said in Luke 10:18, *'I saw Satan fall like lightning from heaven.'*

In the Book of Revelation the third trumpet blast heralded the fall of a great and evil star, blazing like a torch as it hurtled from the heavens to earth. Its impact resulted in the poisoning of the fresh water supply and the deaths of many people (Revelation 8:10).

Interestingly some bible scholars take this star to be symbolic of a political entity, or an influential governor. The poisoning of the waters is also considered to be symbolic of the poisoning of laws which are the springs of civil liberty, poisoned by an autocratic system.[1]

It is also interesting to note that after the fifth trumpet blast an evil star is seen falling from the heavens to earth upon which it is given the key to open the bottomless pit — to unleash hell itself. To have this ability the star has to be a human or a being of some description. It cannot refer to a literal star. (Revelation 9)

The fact that the star-like rock hit Europe, causing immense devastation, led me to see an association with the flag of the European Union.

The stars represent a demonically inspired federation of nations called the European Union. The star-like rock in my vision therefore has to do with a confederation of states that is the context for the emergence of the end-times version of the Roman Empire and the rise of the Antichrist.

The impression of darkness and destruction I had as I watched this part of the vision play out confirmed that the EU is neither morally neutral nor benevolent in the eyes of God.

The rock entering from outside the earthly realm highlighted that the EU was being influenced by dark spiritual forces.

The location of the rock's impact in Europe further confirmed that the Lord was warning about the immense evil that is being unleashed through the EU.

The timing of the vision itself was significant because it came during the drafting of the Maastricht Treaty in 1991 — a Treaty that ratified the creation of the EU.

I wondered at the time if this was a trumpet blast warning about the physical birth of the Antichrist within the European Union.

I didn't know for sure.

But what I did know was, that what had come upon the earth at that time had its source in the demonic principalities and powers in the heavenly realms.

And I knew for sure that this meant the rise of the Antichrist system.

This does not mean however that the Antichrist is only bound to the European Union system. Revelation 12:9 tells us that 'all the people who belong to this world' will be deceived. As the rock struck in my vision, the whole earth shuddered and shockwaves could be felt far beyond the borders of Europe.

This was symbolic of the impact spreading out and crossing over into other political institutions and religious bodies around the world. One obvious place affected — and indeed infected by the Antichrist system — is the United Nations — as I point out in my book *Trumpet Blast Warning*.

The European Union is therefore like an epicentre, a haven, or an incubator. What happens in Europe will be a catalyst for darkness that has global ramifications. In fact Europe is now the perfect soil for the Antichrist to take root and flourish like a foul and devastating weed, blighting the whole globe.

In case you think this is the stuff of fantasy, look at this official EU poster from 1992:

The building in the picture represents the EU Parliament in Strasbourg. The illustration is modelled on the unfinished Tower of Babel — a tower that was built out of idolatry and blasphemy in the time of Nimrod, when the whole world had one language. This is why the tagline of the picture says 'Europe — many tongues, one voice' (a clear reference to Babel).[2]

This is surely a demonically inspired image.

In case you're in any doubt, look at the EU stars hovering over the parliament building. They are unusually inverted to form a common symbol associated with Satanism.

Seen in this light, it is amazing how most people — including Christians — are fast asleep and completely unaware of the darkness spreading throughout Europe.

We need a trumpet blast warning!

If you live outside Europe, don't switch off. Don't be complacent. The impact of the dark rock will not be restricted to the geographical boundaries of Europe. The EU is expanding all the time. It will eventually expand into, and become part of a global government, whether that is through the European Union as it now stands or through the morphing of the EU into another entity. This I believe is more likely to be the case. But of course only time will tell.

The important thing is for us to wake up and to see with prophetic eyes what is clearly going on as darkness, a thick darkness, covers the earth (Isaiah 60:1-3).

This is not a time to be sleeping.

This is even more urgent when you consider the fourth part of my vision sequence, in which I saw a tower of gold that embodied the spirit of man.

Here's the description again:

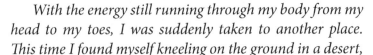

With the energy still running through my body from my head to my toes, I was suddenly taken to another place. This time I found myself kneeling on the ground in a desert, my knees in the sand that was all around me.

I saw a giant, cylindrical, gold tower before me. It felt as if it had the spirit of man in it as it grew taller and taller before me. I watched as brick by brick the tower was assembled at an incredible pace and as it grew taller and taller I ascended with it, flying up and up with every round of golden bricks that was laid in quick succession.

Suddenly the tower came to an abrupt stop as it was completed.

I now found myself hovering at the top of the tower which had ascended far above the clouds.

I saw that the tower which now embodied the collective spirits of many people — an indecipherable number — had become like God. I was totally perplexed by this and did not understand what it meant.

When I saw this golden tower it reminded me of the Tower of Babel.

Eight years later, in 1999, the European Parliament building in Strasbourg was completed. Incredibly, as I mentioned earlier, the official EU poster depicted it as the biblical construction, in an allusion to the famous 1563 painting, 'The Tower of Babel' by Pieter Brueghel.

In the book of Genesis, chapter 11, the story is told how the people of earth were of one language, and after coming to Babylon they settled there. A people of one single mind they decided to build a great city with a tower whose pinnacle would extend into the heavens. God divided that people by confusing their speech and thus ended its unholy construction (Genesis 11:1-4 NKJV).

*Now the whole earth had one language and one speech. And it came to pass, as they journeyed from the east, that they found a plain in the land of Shinar, and they dwelt there. Then they said to one another, "Come, let us make bricks and bake them thoroughly." They had brick for stone, and they had asphalt for mortar. And they said, "Come, let us build ourselves a city, **and a tower whose top is in the heavens**; let us make a name for ourselves, lest we be scattered abroad over the face of the whole earth."*

It is impossible not to sense a deliberate and defiant re-enactment of the sin of Babel in the design and construction of the EU Parliament.

But such pride always comes before a fall.

This is where I believe the sand in my vision is significant.

The sand in which I knelt when I saw this tower was reminiscent of the parable Jesus told in Matthew 7:26-27:

'Everyone who hears these sayings of Mine, and does not do them, **will be like a foolish man who built his house on the sand:** and the rain descended, the floods came, and the winds blew and beat on that house; and it fell. And great was its fall.'

God is not mocked.

What the EU has built is built on sand.

It will face His judgment in due time.

Europe has a history of Christianity. During the time of the Reformation in the sixteenth century nearly three quarters of the population of Europe were Bible believing, Christ-loving Christians.

Europe has an extraordinary history and legacy of Christianity. Just consider the art and literature that arose from the medieval and Reformation era in Europe. It was predominantly Christian and Biblical in content.

We have heard the teaching of Jesus.

We have listened to His words.

Yet Europe has drifted and departed from them.

So what Europe has built is built on sand

When the floods come and the winds blow and beat upon the 'EU house' it will fall — and great and mighty will be that fall.

This will tragically affect the lives of millions and millions of

Europeans.

Remember that sand in the Bible is also symbolic of people. Many people groups and nations surround the 'tower of the EU'. There are approximately 500 million people under the growing dictatorship of the European Union, although as I have already stated the EU's influence reaches far beyond the peoples of Europe.

The speed in which the tower was built in my vision showed how quickly the European Union will rise and assume power.

The golden bricks represented the wealth stolen from the people through taxes used to resource the European Union beast.

Finally the tower that embodied the spirit of man extending up through the heavens and becoming like God represented the pride of man and the belief that man can ascend above the throne of God and obtain godhood through an earthly kingdom.

This pride is the spirit of the Antichrist.

1. Matthew Henry, *Commentary on the Whole Bible Volume VI*, (Acts to Revelation), 1658

2. Jason Carter, *Trumpet Blast Warning*, (Trumpet Blast Publishing, 2014), 110-111

Chapter 7

Increasing Light

Chapter 7

Increasing Light

In the third sequence of my vision I saw what I can only describe as an enthralling picture of the church as it is truly called to be — the church that will rise as we draw nearer and nearer to the climax of history.

Here is what I saw:

Immediately afterwards I moved location and saw the Holy Spirit residing in the hearts of the true saints of God. This was a source of great joy and comfort to my soul. The Holy Spirit was not just present with these people. He literally embodied them.

The eyes of these saints were so consumed with the indwelling presence of the Holy Spirit that they glowed with what appeared to be the eyes of Christ himself.

Their eyes were connected directly to their spirits. Christ was visible in their eyes because He resided so deeply in the spirits of these fully surrendered Christians.

These people walked as though in slow motion throughout the earth — gently, humbly and gracefully showing Jesus Christ to the world in good deeds.

Some were silent and inconspicuous, while others were more vocal and obvious.

Each was as vital as the other.

There was no division between male and female, or between those of great rank and those of lesser rank.

All this felt totally out of place and irrelevant among these Christ-consumed people.

This was a great source of comfort to me because I was painfully aware that as the darkness grew stronger and stronger in Europe, and indeed spread from Europe, the church as it is now would need to change radically.

If the darkness is to be confronted effectively, then the church will need to be more and more filled with the light of the glory of God seen in the face of his Son, Jesus Christ.

As the prophet Isaiah once declared (60:1-3):

> *'Arise, shine, for your light has come,*
> *and the glory of the Lord rises upon you.*
> *See, darkness covers the earth*
> *and thick darkness is over the peoples,*
> *but the Lord rises upon you*
> *and his glory appears over you.*
> *Nations will come to your light,*
> *and kings to the brightness of your dawn.'*

The call upon the church is to arise and shine as thick darkness covers the earth.

It is a call for the people of God to be overshadowed more and more with the glory of God, which is the Holy Spirit.

So it was deeply comforting to me when God showed me in my vision sequence this image of the Holy Spirit residing in the hearts of the true saints of God. I knew straight away that these were end-time believers, strong in faith and might, empowered by the Holy Spirit to preach the Gospel throughout the earth during a time of great upheaval and persecution.

They will not waver in their commitment and loyalty because they are completely full of the Holy Spirit to do great exploits and also to endure terrible suffering for the name of Christ.

The Bible teaches that in the end of days the Holy Spirit will be poured out on everyone, that there will be a persecution of the saints, and that the Gospel will be preached throughout the world.

'In the last days,' God says, 'I will pour out my Spirit upon all people.' (Acts 2:17 NLT)

During this phase of history there will be great tribulation (affliction, distress, and oppression) such as has not been experienced since from the beginning of the world until now — and never will be again.

Thank God these dark days will not last long. As Jesus promised in Matthew 24:21-22 (AMP):

And if those days had not been shortened, no human being would endure and survive, but for the sake of the elect (God's chosen ones) those days will be shortened.

During this time the Gospel will go global and the Kingdom of God will be extended throughout the entire earth (Matthew 24:14 NKJV):

And this gospel of the kingdom will be preached in all the world as a witness to all the nations, and then the end will come.

In other words, in the context of thick darkness, Spirit-filled believers will take the Gospel like torch-bearers to every nation.

Those who live with such Spirit-filled courage and faithfulness will be greatly rewarded in the hereafter.

This brings me to the fifth part of my vision sequence.

I was walking in the spirit through the earth after the rapture of the saints and after the coming of the Lord Jesus.

The people walking around me were clothed in bright white garments right down to their feet.

They moved about as though in slow motion and it looked to me as if they were not walking but rather gliding two or three inches above the ground. I wasn't sure exactly how they moved.

These people were in total peace and contentment, with clear hearts and minds. They did not look either to the left or the right but appeared to be fixing their gaze straight ahead. They seemed to me to be engaged in some kind of task but I had no idea what this was.

These were the redeemed of God, whose garments had been washed in the precious blood of Jesus.

Here I saw the church after the Rapture of the saints and the return of the Lord Jesus Christ.

What a wonderful prospect this is!

Those who have fought the good fight during a time of unprecedented tribulation will receive their reward.

They will be caught up in the air to meet the returning Christ.

They will be given new resurrection bodies and clothed in the pure white garments of heaven.

As the Book of Revelation promises (3:4-5a, NKJV), '*...and they shall walk with Me in white, for they are worthy. He who overcomes shall be clothed in white garments.*'

The city of God, the New Jerusalem, will be their home. As I saw in my vision:

As I turned the corner I looked up beyond the people and I saw in the horizon far away what appeared to be the Holy City of God in the sky. The New Jerusalem was descending down out of the heavens with a great light as of the sun. This light was emanating from within it. The city itself gave the light. There was no sun to illuminate it. The light was golden.

Indeed, the city itself appeared to be made of gold. Near the centre of the city, which seemed symmetrical in design, a great golden domed building stood majestic and tall above the rest and glistened in its own light.

What a contrast to the thick darkness spreading across the earth in our day.

Here is the City of God, filled with beautiful and brilliant light, coming down from heaven to earth.

This is precisely what the Apostle John saw in the Book of Revelation (21:23-24, NKJV):

*The city had no need of the sun or of the moon to shine in it, for the glory of God illuminated it. The Lamb is its light. And the nations of those who are saved **shall walk in its light**, and the kings of the earth bring their glory and honour into it.*

This is what lies in store for those who are filled with the Spirit of God, who are clothed with his white light of purity, and who minister the glory of God.

These are the redeemed of the Lord.

The promise God gives to them is that he will snatch them out of the thick darkness and great persecution in earth's final years and days.

As the Apostle Paul put it in 1 Thessalonians 4:17:

Then we who are alive and remain shall be caught up together with them in the clouds to meet the Lord in the air. And thus we shall always be with the Lord.

And in 1 Corinthians 15:51-52 he wrote:

Behold, I tell you a mystery: We shall not all sleep, but we shall all be changed — in a moment, in the twinkling of an eye, at the last trumpet.

Importantly, it should be noted that not all the saints will avoid persecution. Many believers will endure great suffering and receive martyrdom before the rapture occurs. Revelation 20:4 says: *Then I saw the souls of those who had been beheaded for their witness to Jesus and for the word of God, who had not worshiped the beast or his image, and had not received his mark on their foreheads or on their hands. And they lived and reigned with Christ for a thousand years.*

The living and the dead in Christ are promised a great reward. In fact the Scriptures tell us that those who are faithful even to the death will receive the crown of life! (Revelation 2:10)

Not only will the saints be taken out of this dark world through death or through rapture. They will also live in the radiant City of God.

This City will come down from heaven when the present age comes to a close and the darkness has left the planet. When Satan and his fallen angels have been judged, the earth and the heavens will be purged and changed.

Then the City of God will descend to this redeemed planet. As John saw in his vision (Revelation 21: 1-4 NKJV):

Now I saw a new heaven and a new earth, for the first heaven and the first earth had passed away. Also there was no more sea. Then I,

John, saw the holy city, New Jerusalem, coming down out of heaven from God, prepared as a bride adorned for her husband. And I heard a loud voice from heaven saying, "Behold, the tabernacle of God is with men, and He will dwell with them, and they shall be His people. God Himself will be with them and be their God. And God will wipe away every tear from their eyes; there shall be no more death, nor sorrow, nor crying. There shall be no more pain, for the former things have passed away.

This City will not be illuminated by lamps or by sunlight.

It will be lit up by the glory of God.

As we read in Revelation 21:23-24:

The city had no need of the sun or of the moon to shine in it, for the glory of God illuminated it. The Lamb is its light. And the nations of those who are saved shall walk in its light, and the kings of the earth bring their glory and honour into it.

This is the promised reward for those saints who allow the Holy Spirit to reside in their hearts and who shine like bright stars in this dark and wicked generation.

The City of God is coming and its inhabitants will be the redeemed of the Lord — saints in whom the Holy Sprit has resided and will forever reside.

Chapter 8

The Blessed Trinity

Chapter 8

The Blessed Trinity

It has been pointed out in the past that there's a **difference between a belief and a conviction.**

A belief is something you hold.

A conviction is something that holds you.

One of the most precious doctrines to true Christian believers is the doctrine of the Trinity. This is the teaching that God is three divine persons in one substance or being. God is Father, Son and Holy Spirit.

This is a pivotal and vitally important doctrine of the Christian church.

For authentic believers, it is a conviction more than just a belief.

In the end-times, this conviction will be of paramount importance. True Christians will worship the Father, through Jesus, in the power of the Holy Spirit.

They will adore, honour and venerate the Trinity.

Indeed, they will have intimate communion with the Triune God in heaven while they are enduring great trials here on the earth.

This will be an indelible mark of genuine Christianity in the last days — a conviction that God is Three-in-One and One-in-Three, and an experiential communion with the Triune God in their spirits.

Such believers will not compromise when it comes to this indispensable doctrine.

This brings me to the sixth part of my vision sequence in which I experienced the Blessed Trinity in heaven:

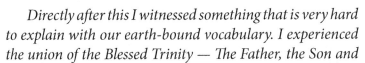

Directly after this I witnessed something that is very hard to explain with our earth-bound vocabulary. I experienced the union of the Blessed Trinity — The Father, the Son and the Holy Spirit.

I didn't see their individual forms but I felt their presence in a deeply intimate way — up close, as though in front of my face, as close as a friend is to a friend.

It was as though I saw the Blessed Trinity — The Father, the Son and the Holy Spirit and I was somehow in complete and direct fellowship with them and that it appeared perfectly natural to be so.

It didn't feel like anything out of the ordinary.

I was quite at ease.

The three persons of the Trinity were happy that I was present with them. Their oneness with each other was so complete.

They appeared to me like crystal clear blue water that contained countless thoughts — a swirling expanse in which the Father, the Son and the Holy Spirit spoke with one another continuously and without end.

My finite, human mind was unable to contain the extremely intense sensation that was now passing through it.

It appeared to me I was being so totally submerged and saturated that I was no longer able to contain the experience within my mind.

It felt like I was somehow drowning in it but I was not in any way fearful.

This meeting with God flooded my mind.

I was experiencing what felt like a torrent and holding on for dear life lest I might be swept away by this great and wonderful experience and lose myself in it forever.

I witnessed the One True God as three individual persons but yet they were ONE and the SAME!

This was an unfathomable and glorious mystery to me.

What shall we say about this part of the vision?

The first thing to underscore is that the Holy Spirit was reminding me that God is Three-in-One.

He was reinforcing in me the importance of communing with the God who is Three Persons, One Being.

Ever since the beginning of church history, this has been one of the hallmarks of genuine Christianity.

The early Christian Creeds (confessions of faith) encouraged us to believe and declare that God is Father, Son and Holy Spirit.

The Athanasian Creed reads thus:

We worship one God in Trinity, and Trinity in Unity; neither confounding the Persons; nor dividing the Essence, for there is one Person of the Father; another of the Son; and another of the Holy Spirit. But the Godhead of the Father, of the Son, and of the Holy Ghost, is all one...

The Apostles Creed encourages us to worship the Father, the Son and the Holy Spirit:

> *I believe in God,*
> *the **Father** almighty,*
> *Creator of heaven and earth,*
> *and in Jesus Christ, his only **Son**, our Lord,*
> *who was conceived by the Holy Spirit,*
> *born of the Virgin Mary,*
> *suffered under Pontius Pilate,*
> *was crucified, died and was buried;*
> *he descended into hell;*
> *on the third day he rose again from the dead;*
> *he ascended into heaven,*
> *and is seated at the right hand of God the Father almighty;*
> *from there he will come to judge the living and the dead.*
> *I believe in the **Holy Spirit**,*
> *the holy catholic Church,*
> *the communion of saints,*
> *the forgiveness of sins,*
> *the resurrection of the body,*
> *and life everlasting.*
> *Amen.*

So does the *Nicene Creed*, the profession of faith believed and accepted by all the denominations of the Christian church:

> *We believe in one God,*
> *the Father, the Almighty,*
> *maker of heaven and earth,*
> *of all that is,*
> *seen and unseen.*
> *We believe in one Lord, Jesus Christ,*
> *the only Son of God,*
> *eternally begotten of the Father,*
> *God from God, Light from Light,*
> *true God from true God,*

begotten, not made,
of one Being with the Father;
through him all things were made...
We believe in the Holy Spirit,
the Lord, the giver of life,
who proceeds from the Father and the Son,
who with the Father and the Son is worshipped and glorified,
who has spoken through the prophets.

You can see from these three creeds that the Christian church has held on to the conviction about God's Triune character since the beginning.

This is because Christians know that even though the word 'Trinity' isn't used in the Bible, everything in the Bible points to the fact that God is Three-in-One and One-in-Three.

When God created the earth, all three persons of God were involved.

This is why God says 'let **US** make man in our own image', rather than 'I will make man in my own image.'

As early as Genesis 1:27 we see the communion and the conversation of the God who is three persons.

This is further confirmed by the fact that in the very act of creation God makes the world with the help of the Holy Spirit (who hovers like a great bird over the pre-creation void) and by bringing all things into being through the power of his Word (Jesus, who is the Word).

Here the Father, the Son and the Holy Spirit work in a glorious synergy and unity to form the heavens and the earth for human beings to inhabit.

Then in the declaration uttered by the Jewish people every day since the time of Moses there is a clue to the Trinitarian nature of God.

'Hear, O Israel, the Lord your God, the Lord is one.'

This is an extraordinary statement. The Hebrew word used for 'Lord' in the last part of that statement is Elohim.

This is a plural word!

It could be translated 'divine beings'!

'The Lord is one' is then an apparent contradiction. 'The Lord(s) is one.'

How can a plural word be described as singular reality?

The only answer we can give is that the Jewish people are giving honour to the God who is Three-in-One without realizing it!

These words from Deuteronomy 6:8, known as the Shema Yisrael, are uttered by the Jewish people at the beginning and end of their daily morning and evening prayer services. They are an unconscious confession of a truth that they deny — that God is three persons, one being!

How precious is the doctrine of the Blessed Trinity!

What a miracle it is, and what a mystery!

If this idea seems too difficult to grasp then we need to consider that if God is really God then he is far beyond our human and finite minds to understand Him completely!

As the theologians of the early church used to say, 'a comprehended God is no God at all.'

In other words, if you can understand Him, then you have limited Him to the contours of your thinking. If you've done that then He's no longer infinite, He's finite.

Therefore He is no longer God!

And that makes sense.

So there are aspects of this doctrine that are very hard to grasp and perhaps which we will never grasp this side of heaven.

But just because we cannot understand it does not mean that it is not so.

Job 36:26 declares: *'How great is God—beyond our understanding!'*

The Apostle Paul writes, *'Now I know in part'* (1 Corinthians 13:12).

The first followers of Jesus, including the Apostle Paul, always spoke about the three persons of God without compromising their oneness.

They may not have used the word 'Trinity' but they certainly gave voice to what we now call the Doctrine of the Trinity.

Here is the Apostle Paul's standard benediction in 2 Corinthians 13:14:

May the grace of the Lord Jesus Christ, and the love of God, and the fellowship of the Holy Spirit be with you all.

Here he talks about Jesus, God and the Holy Spirit.

That's the Trinity!

We have to remember here that Paul's thinking was irrevocably transformed at his conversion. He saw the ascended Jesus in the heavens and heard him speak to him. That changed everything for Paul! If Jesus was at the throne of God in heaven, then Jesus was and is Lord. He is Adonai, which means 'Lord', and is a title for God.

When Paul was converted he confessed Jesus as Lord and he was also baptised in the Holy Spirit.

So now he had two more persons to think about, in addition to the God whom he was calling 'Abba, Father'. No wonder Paul thereafter spoke about God as the Three-in-One and One-in-Three, even if he never explicitly used the word 'Trinity.'

And he wasn't alone. The Apostle John did the same. 1 John 5:7 says: *'for there are three that bear witness in heaven: the Father, the Word, and the Holy Spirit; and these three are one.'* (NKJV) *'The*

Word' spoken of in this passage is Jesus Christ. (see John 1:1-18)

From the earliest days of Christianity, Jesus Christ was acknowledged as God. This is evident from the fact that believers worshipped Jesus. They gave the same kind of devotion and adoration to Jesus as they did to God Almighty. This did not mean that they replaced God with Jesus in their worship. Rather, they understood that the Father, the Son and the Holy Spirit were the three persons of God and that each deserved the highest praise.

In case you still need convincing, here are the last recorded words of Jesus before he ascended into heaven (Matthew 28:18-20, emphasis mine):

*'All authority in heaven and on earth has been given to me. Therefore go and make disciples of all nations, baptising them **in the name of the Father and of the Son and of the Holy Spirit**, and teaching them to obey everything I have commanded you. And surely I am with you always, to the very end of the age.'*

Why is all this so important?

The Bible makes it clear that in the end times there will be a great amount of demonic deception — false teaching deriving from lying spirits designed to disable Christians in the last days.

The Doctrine of the Trinity is already being attacked and it must be protected and proclaimed at all costs.

Any religious person, church or group that does not honour the conviction that God is Three-in-One and One-in-Three is in gross error and has erred from the path of truth.

To stray from a Trinitarian faith grounded in the Bible and the creeds is to stray into falsehood and into the lie promulgated by the Antichrist spirit pervading the world today.

Offshoots of Christianity such as the Jehovah Witnesses and The Church of Jesus Christ of the Latter Day Saints (Mormonism) are examples of such groups. It is vitally important to understand that such movements are not a part of the Christian church in any way. They are impostors and false teachers. Their beliefs do not lead to eternal salvation and their followers are sorely deceived.

Jesus said: *'Most assuredly, I say to you, he who does not enter the sheepfold by the door, but climbs up some other way, the same is a thief and a robber. But he who enters by the door [Jesus] is the shepherd of the sheep.'* (John 10:1-2 NKJV)

Jesus Christ is the only Door to heaven.

He is the only one through whom we can be saved.

He is the one and only Son of God.

Along with the person of the Father and the person of the Holy Spirit, the Son is to be worshipped and glorified forever.

So hold fast to the Doctrine of the Trinity.

When you think of God, think of Him as Three-in-One and One-in-Three.

Accept the invitation to commune with the Three Persons of God in your spirit.

Enjoy their company.

As my vision shows, they enjoy ours!

Chapter 9

The Wonderful Cross

Chapter 9

The Wonderful Cross

The seventh part of my vision took place at the Cross of Christ. There I saw his appalling suffering and the dreadful price paid for our sin and salvation.

This is what I saw:

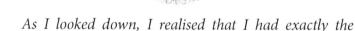

As I looked down, I realised that I had exactly the same vantage point as Christ himself. He was suspended and cruelly transfixed in a standing position on the Cross, looking down at his surroundings. It felt to me as if I was looking through my precious Saviour's eyes.

Everything seemed grey to me — no colour at all, only shades of grey.

Clouds and smoke seemed to be billowing about Golgotha's hill, swirling and twisting all around me in the air.

I slowly turned my gaze to the left and then to the right, looking at the outstretched arms of my Saviour — the arms that had brought so much comfort and healing to so many.

His muscles were taut.

His skin was pale, as though His flesh had been drained of blood.

As I gazed through the Saviour's eyes, my soul was filled with an immense and overwhelming sorrow.

I felt what He felt — the grief that He was enduring and the appalling and repulsive sin of the world that He was bearing.

In my heart I knew with crushing certainty that every wicked deed committed from the beginning of time to that dreadful day was laid upon His shoulders.

The one who had never sinned was carrying our sin.

He was carrying my sin.

In this part of the vision I looked through the eyes of Christ on that dark and terrible day.

Surrounding the hill of Calvary were dark and swirling clouds and billowing smoke. This symbolised the violent storm of sinfulness as it gathered from all the ages, culminating in one place upon Calvary's hill on that day.

The encircling clouds also reminded me of events recorded in the Gospels of Matthew, Mark and Luke where darkness covered the land during the time of the crucifixion (Matthew 27:45-46, NKJV):

Now from the sixth hour until the ninth hour there was darkness over all the land. And about the ninth hour Jesus cried out with a loud voice, saying, "Eli, Eli, lama sabachthani?" that is, "My God, My God, why have You forsaken Me?"'

The extreme sense of sorrow and agony of soul Christ felt as he hung on the cross for the sin of humanity was totally immeasurable to me.

However, we do get a glimpse into the agony suffered by Christ in the hours leading up to his crucifixion. *'And being in agony, He prayed more earnestly.'* (Luke 22:44 NKJV)

In Matthew 26:36-38 this is spelled out in more detail:

Then Jesus came with them to a place called Gethsemane, and said to the disciples, "Sit here while I go and pray over there." And He took with Him Peter and the two sons of Zebedee, and He began to be **sorrowful** *and* **deeply distressed.** *Then He said to them, "***My soul is exceedingly sorrowful, even to death.*** Stay here and watch with Me."*

The Bible also very powerfully and memorably describes the sufferings and sorrows of Christ in the Book of Isaiah chapter 53 — one of the great Messianic prophecies of the Old Testament:

Who has believed our report?
And to whom has the arm of the Lord been revealed?
For He shall grow up before Him as a tender plant,
And as a root out of dry ground.
He has no form or comeliness;
And when we see Him,
There is no beauty that we should desire Him.
He is despised and rejected by men,
A Man of sorrows and acquainted with grief.
And we hid, as it were, our faces from Him;
He was despised, and we did not esteem Him.

Surely He has borne our griefs
And carried our sorrows;
Yet we esteemed Him stricken,
Smitten by God, and afflicted.
But He was wounded for our transgressions,
He was bruised for our iniquities;
The chastisement for our peace was upon Him,
And by His stripes we are healed.
All we like sheep have gone astray;

We have turned, every one, to his own way;
And the Lord has laid on Him the iniquity of us all.

He was oppressed and He was afflicted,
Yet He opened not His mouth;
He was led as a lamb to the slaughter,
And as a sheep before its shearers is silent,
So He opened not His mouth.
He was taken from prison and from judgment,
And who will declare His generation?
For He was cut off from the land of the living;
For the transgressions of My people He was stricken.
And they made His grave with the wicked—
But with the rich at His death,
Because He had done no violence,
Nor was any deceit in His mouth.

Yet it pleased the Lord to bruise Him;
He has put Him to grief.
When You make His soul an offering for sin,
He shall see His seed, He shall prolong His days,
And the pleasure of the Lord shall prosper in His hand.
He shall see the labour of His soul, and be satisfied.
By His knowledge My righteous Servant shall justify many,
For He shall bear their iniquities.
Therefore I will divide Him a portion with the great,
And He shall divide the spoil with the strong,
Because He poured out His soul unto death,
And He was numbered with the transgressors,
And He bore the sin of many,
And made intercession for the transgressors."

It seemed then that the Holy Spirit wanted me to enter into a deeper revelation of the Cross.

He wanted me to experience a heartfelt empathy with the sorrows and sufferings of Christ at Calvary.

He wanted me to get a clearer picture of what Christ endured and why he suffered so.

Friend, I wonder, do you know why he suffered? He suffered to bring you back into relationship with God. He suffered so that you can partake of His life here on earth now and also in the life hereafter. He suffered to relieve you of the guilt of wrongdoing.

If you are reading this and you are not in relationship with God, now would be a perfect opportunity to speak with Him. You could say something like this:

"Lord God, I am so sorry for going my own way. Thank you God that because of Jesus death I receive perfect forgiveness. Jesus, please come into my life today and be my Saviour and my Lord."

Once you have done this get hold of a bible and begin by reading the Gospels, also find a Bible believing church in your area to continue the exciting journey you have just begun.

Now returning back to the interpretation. This all led into the eighth and final part of my vision which involved the thrusting of the Roman spear into Christ's side, the subsequent calling out to 'David', seeing the house of David with the generations from King David to Christ and from Christ to today, and lastly being in the family of Christ.

Back in 1991 this seemed to be the most peculiar part of the vision and the most difficult for me to comprehend. However it holds a profound and significant end-time prophetic message.

Here is the first stage of this eighth part of the vision sequence once again:

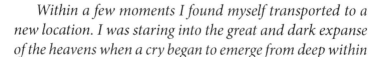

Within a few moments I found myself transported to a new location. I was staring into the great and dark expanse of the heavens when a cry began to emerge from deep within my heart. It was a name.

'David! David! David!' I shouted.

As I spoke this name in some anguish of soul, I felt a pain in my right side.

I clutched my side in agony.

As I did, I saw the lifeless body of the Saviour laying on the ground. A Roman legionary had moments earlier, thrust the blade of his spear into the Lord's side. It was as if he had pierced me as well. As I felt the pain, I was sorely distressed and grieved in my spirit that the Saviour's body had been so mistreated and abused.

Once again I cried out.

'David! David! David!'

As I continued to shout, I saw in the deepest and remotest darkness of the heavens an extraordinary house emerge. It was gleaming with gold and encircled by swirling and radiant clouds of glory.

I went on uttering the name, 'David,' my voice becoming softer and less urgent as I gazed upon this wondrous site.

Then I understood: this was the House of David — the house from which Christ himself was descended.

I was filled with awe.

The house was small, but beautiful and majestic.

Then I saw generations of Jewish people, and Gentile people filing out from this far away house and proceeding in two separate lines through the heavens until they reached the place where the resurrected Christ was standing, clothed in white with arms outstretched.

When all these peoples reached Christ they then parted and stretched out in different directions, until they reached the present time.

I saw that not only had Christ's cruel death rescued human beings from sin and the agony of being separated from the Father. It had also brought both Jew and Gentile together into one family, God's family here on earth.

I saw that anyone who called upon the name of the Lord Jesus Christ in repentance, whether Jew or Gentile, would now become a part of the family line of Jesus, beginning at the Cross.

I was filled with awe.

The strangest thing about this part of the vision was the fact that I instinctively called out the name 'David' deep from within my spirit as I felt the spear being thrust in Christ's side. I did not call out 'Jesus' as would normally have been my first inclination.

It is significant that I called out 'David'. As I uttered the name of David it was as though I was uttering the name of the Lord. Those two names were to me in that moment inseparably linked together and as I repeated the name 'David' the glorious vision of the house of David opened up before me.

Many years later and only after the dream vision of 2009 did I come to understand that the piercing of Christ's side and the House of David were powerfully and inextricably linked together in an Old Testament prophecy. Before then I had not connected this.

The link between the house of David and the piercing of Christ's side can be found in a prophecy concerning the Messiah Jesus Christ in the book of Zechariah (12:10) which reads:

*And I will pour on the **house of David** and on the inhabitants of Jerusalem the Spirit of grace and supplication; **then they will look on Me whom they pierced.** Yes, they will mourn for Him as one mourns for his only son, and grieve for Him as one grieves for a firstborn."*

This passage is a direct reference to Jesus the Messiah, who was pierced in his side as he hung upon the cross in the final stages of the crucifixion.

The Gospel of John records this moment (John 19:34, NKJV):

*One of the soldiers **pierced His side with a spear,** and immediately blood and water came out.*

That this is a fulfilment of Zechariah's prophecy is confirmed in John 19:37 when directly after the soldier has thrust his lance into Christ's dying body, John writes:

*And again another Scripture says, **"They shall look on Him whom they pierced."***

To whom does this word 'they' refer?

In the original context it refers to the Jewish people.

This is really important. In the last part of my vision sequence the emphasis was very much on the family of Christ. This end-time family is to be made up of both Jewish and Gentile believers in Jesus. In other words, the end-times church will be noted for its unity.

Here is the Apostle Paul's vision of the church in Ephesians 2:11-22:

Therefore, remember that formerly you who are Gentiles by birth and called 'uncircumcised' by those who call themselves 'the circumcision' (which is done in the body by human hands) — remember that at that time you were separate from Christ, excluded from citizenship in Israel and foreigners to the covenants of the promise, without hope and without God in the world. But now in Christ Jesus you who once were far away have been brought near by the blood of Christ.

For he himself is our peace, who has made the two groups one and has destroyed the barrier, the dividing wall of hostility, by setting aside in his flesh the law with its commands and regulations. His purpose was to create in himself one new humanity out of the two, thus making peace, and in one body to reconcile both of them to God through the cross, by which he put to death their hostility. He came and preached peace to you who were far away and peace to those who were near. For through him we both have access to the Father by one Spirit.

Consequently, you are no longer foreigners and strangers, but fellow citizens with God's people and also members of his household, built on the foundation of the apostles and prophets, with Christ Jesus himself as the chief cornerstone.

In him the whole building is joined together and rises to become a holy temple in the Lord. And in him you too are being built together to become a dwelling in which God lives by his Spirit.

What a glorious picture of the church!

As a result of Christ's blood, the walls of division between Jew and Gentile have come crashing down. Now, instead of being two divided races at war with each other, Jews and Gentiles can both have access to Abba Father through Jesus and in the power of the Holy Spirit. Thanks to the Cross of Christ, people of different and even hostile races can find peace with God and with each other and learn to live as the family of Christ in the harmonious household of the church.

This then is why I saw the line of Jewish and Gentile believers filing out from the House of David right down to the present day.

This is why I cried out 'David'.

This is why my vision ended with the family of Christ in heaven and earth, the brotherhood of Jesus and the seed of Abraham.

The Holy Spirit wanted to show me the extraordinary end-times church that God is raising up on the earth — a church where there will be no division between Jew and Gentile, and where both in Christ will celebrate the legacy from Abraham and Jesus as their Brother.

What this means is that there will be a lifting of the veil from the minds of the Jewish people in the final stages of history.

The Jewish people — those literally and physically descended from the House of David — are going to experience a mighty move of the Holy Spirit.

Suddenly, like Saul of Tarsus on the Damascus Road, they are going to see Jesus.

And they are going to look upon him whom they pierced at Calvary.

When that day comes, Jew and Gentile followers of Jesus, filled with the Holy Spirit and enjoying intimate access to the Father in heaven, will form the kind of church that God has been longing for throughout the last two thousand years.

This church will have a radical unity in which those who formally wouldn't have been seen dead with each other will now be prepared to die for one another.

This day is coming.

It is a day not far off.

It is a day that presages the coming of the Lord Jesus Christ.

That is why the last word cannot be given to my vision but to that of the Apostle John, who declared in Revelation 1:7 (NKJV):

Behold, He is coming with clouds, and every eye will see Him, ***even they who pierced Him.*** *And all the tribes of the earth will mourn because of Him. Even so, Amen.*

Part III

The Application

Chapter 10

Get Ready!

Chapter 10

Get Ready!

*A*t the start of this book I mentioned that after the revelations and visions had finally ceased I was left with a deep sense of emptiness in my spirit. In this final chapter I want to pick up from that moment.

This is how I would describe it: I went from encountering mighty visions to not being able to hear God even in the slightest. It felt to me as though His presence had completely left me; worse still, that He had gone from my spirit forever. Have you ever felt this way? If you have then it is important to remember that we should not always trust our feelings. Often our feelings can be contrary to the truth of God's Word. God clearly says many times that *He will never leave us nor forsake us* (Deuteronomy 31:6; Joshua 1:5; Hebrews 13:5). The certain promises of God always trump our uncertain feelings.

If we need further persuading, there's a reassuring promise in Isaiah 43:2 which reads:

When you go through deep waters, I will be with you. When you go through rivers of difficulty, you will not drown. When you walk through the fire of oppression, you will not be burned up; the flames will not consume you. (Isaiah 43:2)

Isn't it wonderful to know that God promises to be with us

through such difficult times? Our God is not a fair-weather God. No, He sticks with us through the darkest hours and the smallest details of our lives.

Psalm 23 declares that even though you may walk through the valley of the shadow of death, you will fear no evil; God promises to be with you to guide you and to comfort you.

Despite knowing these biblical truths and hearing them mentioned by others who were desperately trying to help, some extremely powerful emotions got the better of me. Consequently I descended into a prolonged time of the deepest and darkest depression.

Utterly Meaningless without Christ

The opening lines of the book of Ecclesiastes became my life's signature verse in this season:

"Meaningless! Meaningless!"
"Utterly meaningless!
Everything is meaningless." (Ecclesiastes 1:2, NIV)

Yet it was in this very place of believing God had become silent and thinking that He had left me, that He was actually revealing a more vital revelation to me. What followed next was as significant as the entire vision experience that preceded it.

Let me summarise that vision experience.

I experienced a waking vision in which I stood in the open universe. It was here that I heard the deafening sound of a trumpet blast warning. I witnessed an evil star-like rock plummet towards and strike central Europe. This was the birthing of the European super state in the form of the European Union.

What followed was terrible persecution and suffering that would extend beyond the borders of Europe and affect the world.

I watched as the EU tower was built and saw how man had

exalted himself above the throne of God.

I saw a brave new church, living in revival fire; in short, a great awakening. I witnessed a people totally in tune and saturated with the Holy Spirit, fearlessly going about the earth proclaiming the message of the gospel despite great tribulation and persecution.

I saw the resurrected saints — those previously dead, and those presently alive — raptured into glory after the Second Coming of our Lord.

I saw the New Jerusalem descending from the clouds, resplendent and with great glory — a city of God teeming with life and light, a home for the saints to dwell and to work, to travel into and out of, to work great wonders in the name of the King, Jesus Christ, the ruler of that city.

I met with Father, Son and Holy Spirit and came to understand firsthand that God was so pleased and happy to dwell and commune with us! I understood that because of His great love for us He treated us as though we are on an equal footing with Him!

I 'travelled' down through history and found myself on Calvary's hill. Here I found myself gazing out through the eyes of Christ and realized with shame that it was my abominable sin and the sins of humanity that caused him to hang there.

Soon after this I had a revelation of the depth of relationship Christians have with Christ, whether Jew or Gentile.

That, in summary, was my vision.

Yet after all this, I now found myself totally bereft of everything. God appeared to me to be silent.

Through this experience of deep loss I came to understand truly that without Christ our lives are, as the writer of Ecclesiastes states, 'utterly meaningless'.

Upon waking every morning I was greeted by this single and hopeless thought. It would repeat continuously throughout each and every day. My only rest from this consuming hopelessness was sleep.

My worldview was completely and irrevocably changed. My mind and my spirit were re-wired so to speak, my 'hard drive' wiped. Daily I cried out to God and daily it seemed as though I received no answer, only the repetitive thoughts of a hopeless life without Him. The pain of it seared deeply into my spirit.

My view of people changed too. Compassion for the lost welled up within me as I saw them living in the utter futility of existence without God.

I remember meeting a homeless alcoholic man in town as I walked home. He approached me and asked for money. I instinctively took hold of his hand and gladly gave him some. An unexpected compassion overflowed like a torrent from deep within me. In that moment I suffered with him. As I looked into his trouble-worn and grateful eyes I experienced a glimpse of Christ looking back at me. Yes, before I would have given him money, but I would not have connected at all with his suffering. I probably would have judged him in my heart too.

I watched as people went about their daily chores and business; they met their friends in the street, they joked and they laughed. And all the while I looked on in wonder. How could they live this life without God, which, as the bible says, is here today and gone tomorrow? Such a life is just a chasing after the wind and utterly meaningless without Him. Such bible verses now held great significance for me. My pain for these people became all-consuming. I empathised deeply with them because I was personally walking in a revelation of a life devoid of God.

Time is Running Out

In my mind's eye these people walked about with large countdown clocks hanging around their necks. Each person's time was set differently. I could see nothing else but these clocks; I couldn't get them out of my mind. All I could see was time running out on every person my eyes met. Tick, tick, tick, tick, tick, tick; each passing second was moving towards the end of their lives and an eternity without God.

Later I learned this is a biblical image. The bible tells us that God knows the exact length of our days: *'You have decided the length of our lives. You know how many months we will live, **and we are not given a minute longer.'*** (Job 14:5 NLT)

However these people were nonchalant about their predicament; they cared little or nothing about their own mortality and worse still they cared nothing for God. I likened it to a man sitting in his lounge, entertained by his television. All around him the house is burning to the ground. He sits there oblivious, laughing at the comedian on the screen, but his laughing turns to choking as he is overcome by the smoke, before finally and tragically being consumed by the flames.

I wanted to run up to these people in the street, to interrupt them and shake them out of their malaise. I wanted to shout at them: 'Time is running out!'

Friends: time is running out for all of us, whether we know Jesus or not. In a mere second we could find that we have passed from this life into the next. We should not make the mistake of believing that we will reach old age either; our life could be taken from us at any time. Jesus warned us of this. He spoke about a man who believed that he would live until he was old. But God said to him, 'You fool! This very night your soul is required of you' (Luke 12:20). James also warns us of this. He tells us that all such boasting is evil (James 4:13-17).

The question is, are we ready? Are we ready to meet the Lord? Are our hearts right before Him? Are we in relationship with Him? Are we doing His will?

Back in 1991 my vision was marked by a powerful trumpet

sound blasting throughout the heavens. As I mentioned earlier in the book the trumpet blast denoted a warning, a warning that trouble was coming upon Europe and the world. It was a warning that the Day of the Lord was fast approaching. It was a warning for us to get ready.

Today it is not hard to see that trouble is on the horizon and in many ways has already arrived on our shores. We only have to watch the news or read the papers and compare these events with scripture to see that the world is careering into all that has been prophesied.

How then should we respond to all this as believers?

Fear Not!

If we know God through His son Jesus Christ these thoughts should not strike fear into our hearts. It should not be a hard or frightening message to grasp but a message received and understood.

The bible tells us that whoever fears has not been perfected in love (1 John 4:18). Perfect love from the Father, the bible tells us, casts out all fear. I wonder friend, do you know this perfect love that proceeds from the Father to you? It's easy to find out if you know it or not. Search your heart. Do you fear the future? Do you fear global turmoil? Do you fear for your own safety or the safety of your children? Are you in denial of the possibility of tribulation? If you are fearful, or in denial then you have not come to fully understand the perfect love of the Father.

When Jesus' followers were afraid He immediately spoke to them saying, *"Take courage, it is I, do not be afraid."* (Matthew 14:27) Today He whispers these same words to you. Through all your fears, no matter what they might be, Jesus says, *"My peace I give to you; not as the world gives do I give to you. Do not let your heart be troubled, nor let it be fearful."* (John 14:27)

Why not take a moment to meditate on these words of Christ to you, **"be not afraid,"** and **"My peace I give to you."** Ask God to reveal His love for you today. A real revelation of His love for you will drive out all fear!

This revelation may or may not come immediately. But persevere! You could continue your quest by searching the bible for verses relating to God being your refuge and your shelter. Psalm 46 is a great starting point. Let's read that chapter with a prayerful and quiet heart now:

God is our refuge and strength,
A very present help in trouble.
Therefore we will not fear,
Even though the earth be removed,
And though the mountains be carried into the midst of the sea;
Though its waters roar and be troubled,
Though the mountains shake with its swelling.

There is a river whose streams shall make glad the city of God,
The holy place of the tabernacle of the Most High.
God is in the midst of her, she shall not be moved;
God shall help her, just at the break of dawn.
The nations raged, the kingdoms were moved;
He uttered His voice, the earth melted.

The Lord of hosts is with us;
The God of Jacob is our refuge.

Come, behold the works of the Lord,
Who has made desolations in the earth.
He makes wars cease to the end of the earth;
He breaks the bow and cuts the spear in two;
He burns the chariot in the fire.

Be still, and know that I am God;
I will be exalted among the nations,
I will be exalted in the earth!

The Lord of hosts is with us;
The God of Jacob is our refuge.

As we receive perfect love from the Father, fear has no hold and we will become emboldened and unrestrained in our zeal for Christ. We will be able to face all persecutions that come our way.

Maybe you are reading this and you are not yet a follower of Jesus.

If that is so, now would be a good time to turn your thoughts towards Him. By humbly submitting yourself to God and asking Jesus to enter your life you can begin on the exciting journey that so many have travelled. By finding peace with God you will become equipped through the revelation of His love for you to not fear, no matter what circumstances you may face now or in the future. But more than this you will find eternal salvation with Him.

Facing the Future with Confidence

So let us not shrink back and ignore these afflictions and tribulations that are coming to us as though they will somehow go away. On the contrary let us rather embrace them, and as the Word of God says, consider it pure joy whenever we face various trials knowing with total assurance that the testing of our faith produces perseverance. The kind of perseverance that comes through these trials is priceless. The bible tells us these trials produce in us a maturity in our faith whereby we lack absolutely nothing (James 1:2-4).

Because the western church has enjoyed such a long period of peace and prosperity the very concept of a coming suffering and persecution seems difficult to accept. Some even reject it. It seems to be at odds with their understanding of scripture. But suffering is at the very heart of the gospel message. It should not then come as a surprise to us.

The apostle Peter writes concerning these things: *"Dear friends, do not be surprised at the fiery ordeal that has come on you to test you, as though something strange were happening to you. But rejoice inasmuch as you participate in the sufferings of Christ, so that you may be overjoyed when his glory is revealed."* (1 Peter 4:12-13) Indeed when we are persecuted because of Christ, Peter tells us that the glorious Spirit of God rests upon us! (1 Peter 4:14)

Furthermore, the apostle Paul explains to us the beautiful outworking that suffering for Christ brings! In suffering for Christ, the very life of Jesus is manifested in our body!

Paul says: *"We are hard-pressed on every side, yet not crushed; we are perplexed, but not in despair; persecuted, but not forsaken; struck down, but not destroyed — always carrying about in the body the dying of the Lord Jesus, that the life of Jesus also may be manifested in our body."* 2 Corinthians 4:8-10 (NKJV)

Imagine that! Through suffering for Christ His supernatural life will be activated within our lives and it will be clear for all to see.

Let us then face these trials head on, no matter how they manifest themselves, and so stand firm in this evil day and we will, as Jesus said, 'win life.' (Luke 21:19)

You see, we can say 'we do not fear' when we are in denial of the disturbing events that are unfolding in our world. We can say 'we stand on the bible's promises' when we are not facing up to the reality of suffering and persecution. But there is no need to hide these things under the carpet as though they somehow contradict the gospel message. The perfect love of God casts out all fear, and fear in the face of all persecution, suffering and certain death.

Our mental processes cannot understand this perfect love from the Father; head knowledge is not enough. This truth must be embraced in our hearts through a revelation that can only come through relationship with Him so that we know it instinctively, beyond our conscious reasoning. When trouble comes then the peace of God that passes all understanding will guard our hearts and minds through Christ Jesus (Philippians 4:7). It will spring forth deep from within us and automatically **WE WILL NOT FEAR!**

Revival and Persecution

In these last days there is coming, and indeed has already begun, a shaking of everything that we hold dear, everything in which we put our trust. One of the worst times in earth's history is beginning. It is time to stop trusting in earthly things, ideas and beliefs. It is time to lose interest in our earthly treasures (Matthew 6:19). It is time to stop putting our trust in politicians from whom there is no lasting help (Psalm 146:3-4). Our trust in these things will not serve us in the face of what is coming. We must throw ourselves completely onto God through His Son Jesus Christ. We will find that when we do we will have absolutely nothing to fear. As the Psalmist exhorts us:

"But when I am afraid, I will put my confidence in you. Yes, I will trust the promises of God. And since I am trusting him, what can mere man do to me?" (Psalm 56:3-4)

In this hour our full reliance must be upon Him and Him alone.

A societal collapse is coming; the warning signs are all around us. This will be triggered by a combination of key factors. For example;

- the continued abandonment of godly morals and values
- an ongoing failure of moral political leadership
- equality and human rights laws
- economic meltdown
- the advancement of Islam
- street riots
- staged crisis events
- and civil and global wars

In case you think I am sounding like a prophet of doom and gloom, I am only reiterating what the bible teaches will happen in the closing stages of world history. It's all detailed in God's Word!

But again I repeat, **WE MUST NOT FEAR**. I cannot emphasise this enough. If we truly know God as our Father and experientially walk in the truths of all that the scriptures tell us, we will by default NOT FEAR. Jesus himself exhorts us not to be afraid as the world becomes rocked by end time calamities. Jesus said: *"When you hear of wars and uprisings, do not be frightened."* (Luke 21:9)

An Anointed Army

God is raising up today an army of Holy Spirit-filled believers just like I saw in my vision experience. These will be Christians so endued with the power and love of Christ that they will valiantly stand against every foe. They will fearlessly proclaim the gospel message in the very worst of circumstances.

Christians not filled and flooded with the Holy Spirit will inevitably and tragically leave the faith in the prophesied great falling away. It will be impossible for them to stand the tests coming against them and the end time church.

Holy Spirit empowerment then is a prerequisite for the end time believer; it is an absolute necessity. This is where the rubber hits the road, so to speak. This is what I believe is the end time revival that many speak of today. It is an army of men, women and children wholly filled and flooded with God himself, doing the works of the Kingdom in the same manner as the early church did. They will be totally surrendered to His will, forsaking all else to follow Christ, even unto death.

This is how Jesus said we must be:

"If anyone desires to be My disciple, let him deny himself [disregard, lose sight of, and forget himself and his own interests] and take up his cross and follow Me [cleave steadfastly to Me, conform wholly to My example in living and, if need be, in dying, also]." Matthew 16:24 (AMP)

These are the disciples the church so desperately needs today. How else will it stand against such moral decline and tyranny?

Jesus told us that as the age draws to a close there would be an increase in wickedness, that sin would be rampant everywhere, that lawlessness would abound (Matthew 24:12). We can see this happening all around us today.

There will come a time soon when the true church of Christ will not be able to remain silent on the issues of moral decay or governmental tyranny closing in around it and society. This is when the church will begin to see a rapid increase in persecution. It will be hated for standing up for what the bible emphatically teaches is wrong and is sin. This of course is why the bible and the Ten Commandments are being removed so rapidly from many institutions in the West. The Word of God testifies that their works are evil.

Jesus explained this. The reason the world hated Jesus then and continues to hate Jesus now is because He testifies that its deeds are evil (John 7:7). In the same way, as the true end time church stands up and testifies against the world it will be hated. Jesus said: *"Everyone will hate you because of me... Stand firm, and you will win life."* (Luke 21:17-19)

We can understand from these verses that the end time revival will not be a utopian society where everything becomes perfect, where all are converted to Christ, where government rules justly, where all live in peace and harmony. This is not a biblical concept of the end times. Remember that Jesus said wide is the gate that leads to destruction and many enter through it, and narrow is the gate and there are few who find it (Matthew 7:13-14).

A utopian era does of course follow Christ's return during what is called the millennial reign (Revelation 20:4-6), and finally after this, when Satan is cast into the lake of fire forever (Revelation 20:10). But a utopian era does not precede these events.

Some understand the verses from Joel 2:28 and Acts 2:17 as evidence for a revival that sweeps the globe in this way: *"In the last days, God says, I will pour out my Spirit on all people. Your sons and daughters will prophesy, your young men will see visions, your old men will dream dreams."* However it is important to remember that the last days referred to in the verse is from the day the Holy Spirit was poured out at Pentecost right up until the second coming of Christ. The Holy Spirit is here referred to as being poured out in stark contrast to the mere drops of rain in Old Testament times. In other words the 'revival' or the pouring out spoken of in these verses has been active since Pentecost. We are not then waiting for revival. More accurately God is waiting for revival! He is waiting for us, His church, to be revived! He is waiting for you and me to draw close to Him!

Back to the Early Church

The early church is our blueprint here. Let's think about that for a moment. Today we would certainly agree that the early church was moving in what we would today call revival fire. Signs and wonders, miracles, visions, dreams, prophecies, angelic visitations, resurrections from the dead, mass conversions, you name it, they were experiencing it. It was every modern day revivalist's dream!

At the same time however, it is important to consider the context in which this 'revival' was taking place (for the early Christians of course it wasn't revival; it was the normal Christian experience). The early church was birthed under the occupation of Rome. They were under a dictatorial Antichrist government and an oppressive religious system. They were constantly under surveillance, tortured, imprisoned, and even martyred for their faith. This was the reality of the revival atmosphere in which they lived and died. Both Holy Spirit empowerment and extreme persecution were operating together at the same time.

This is perfectly illustrated in the life of Stephen the first martyr.

Acts 6:8-15 reads:

*Now Stephen, a man **full of God's grace and power, performed
great wonders and signs** among the people. **Opposition arose,**
however, from members of the Synagogue of the Freedmen...who
began to argue with Stephen. But they could not stand up against the
wisdom the Spirit gave him as he spoke. Then they secretly persuaded
some men to say, "We have heard Stephen speak blasphemous words
against Moses and against God." So they stirred up the people and the
elders and the teachers of the law. They seized Stephen and brought
him before the Sanhedrin. They produced false witnesses, who
testified, "This fellow never stops speaking against this holy place and
against the law...All who were sitting in the Sanhedrin looked intently
at Stephen, **and they saw that his face was like the face of an angel.**"*

Stephen then preached a message to the Sanhedrin under a
powerful anointing from the Holy Spirit. The members of the
Sanhedrin became enraged by this message from the Lord. They
dragged him out of the city and began to stone him. This is
important to note. While Stephen was experiencing this traumatic
persecution which resulted in his death, the scriptures tell us:

*But Stephen, full of the Holy Spirit, looked up to heaven and
saw the glory of God, and Jesus standing at the right hand of God.
"Look," he said, "I see heaven open and the Son of Man standing at
the right hand of God"* (Acts 7:55).

On that day we are told that great persecution broke out against
the church and all the apostles were scattered. Houses were searched
and Christians, both men and women, were dragged off to prison.
However, at the exact same time we are told that those who had
been scattered preached the word everywhere. Philip went down
to a city in Samaria and there he preached with signs and wonders
following. People were set free from demonic oppression and many
paralysed and lame were healed.

**In a time of extreme persecution we are told there was great
joy in the city** (Acts 8:1-8).

All this is a blueprint. The first century church is the model for the twenty first century church. The end time church will endure great persecution under the occupation of a revived Roman empire, a dictatorial Antichrist government. Heavy surveillance, imprisonments in Nazi style concentration camps and beheadings will become commonplace. But simultaneously the end time church will be empowered by the Holy Spirit to accomplish great and wondrous acts just like the early church did. Signs and wonders, miracles, visions, dreams, prophecies, angelic visitations, resurrections from the dead, mass conversions and the like will once again be in abundance. Just like the example I saw in my vision of Chinese Christians being propelled out into the earth during a time of great global upheaval, these Christians will preach the gospel with signs following. But this is not reserved for the Chinese only. The church from every nation will rise up and so impact the earth in this way.

An End Time Wake Up Call

If there is one final message I would like to send, it is this: 'get ready!'

Just as the shofar (trumpet) that is sounded during the Jewish season of teshuvah is a wakeup call to repent and prepare for the Day of Judgement, so I believe the trumpet blast I heard back in 1991 continues to be sounded throughout the heavens for this same purpose.

Its sound calls us to return back to the Lord and to seek His face. Its sound warns us of impending danger. Its sound is intended to draw us towards the Lord. Its sound trumpets out continuously to 'get ready!'

Today Jesus is standing at the door! He is perpetually waiting for us to open it. Oh friend, I wonder can you hear the sound of his nail pierced hands knocking on the door? Can you hear the sound of His voice urgently calling out to you to open it?

Jesus said: *"Behold, I stand at the door and knock; if anyone hears and listens to and heeds My voice and opens the door, I will come in to him and will eat with him, and he [will eat] with Me."* (Revelation 3:20 AMP)

Please note that Jesus is not talking to unbelievers here. He is talking to complacent Christians, to a complacent church. He is talking to 'lukewarm fence-sitters,' precariously balanced between two worlds. Friend, this kind of Christian makes Jesus sick to the stomach. That statement might sound shocking to you, but Jesus said it himself; *"So then, because you are lukewarm, and neither cold nor hot, I will vomit you out of My mouth."* (Revelation 3:16 NKJV)

To think that there are types of Christians that make Jesus sick is tragic. But Jesus makes this distinction time and time again.

It is important that we do not misunderstand the sentiment of Christ here. Our love for the world provokes in Jesus an intense and godly jealousy. His emotional and nauseous reaction is borne out of His great love for us! The scriptures tell us plainly that when we love the world we commit adultery against the Lord and his jealously for us is thus aroused.

James chapter 4 writes: *Adulterers and adulteresses! Do you not know that friendship with the world is enmity with God? "The Spirit who dwells in us yearns jealously."*

So then, rather like a husband feels such anguish in knowing that his beloved wife has been unfaithful to him, so Christ feels the same when we are unfaithful to Him.

Furthermore, also consider the words of Christ as He stands knocking. Jesus said: *"I...will eat with him, and he [will eat] with Me."*

Christ's desire to sit down and share a meal together with us is indicative of close friendship, not chastisement. Jesus longs for us to behold him in the kind of fellowship he enjoyed with his friend John, whom the bible tells us 'Jesus loved' (John 20:2) and who reclined with Christ at the feasting table (John 13:23-25).

Get Your Oil Ready

For me one of the most disturbing stories in the bible can be found in Matthew 25. It follows directly Jesus' prophetic warnings about the signs of the end of the age in the previous chapter.

Here Jesus makes the distinction between committed Christians and complacent Christians.

I am referring to the parable of the ten virgins.

Jesus tells us that five were wise and five were foolish. The wise virgins had enough reserve oil for their lamps to light their way to the wedding feast. The remaining five had oil in their lamps but no reserve. They did not have enough for the whole journey. En route their lamps would burn out and they would become lost in the darkness.

Here's the parable in full from Matthew 25:1-13:

"Then the kingdom of heaven shall be likened to ten virgins who took their lamps and went out to meet the bridegroom. Now five of them were wise, and five were foolish. Those who were foolish took their lamps and took no oil with them, but the wise took oil in their vessels with their lamps. But while the bridegroom was delayed, they all slumbered and slept.

"And at midnight a cry was heard: 'Behold, the bridegroom is coming; go out to meet him!' Then all those virgins arose and trimmed their lamps. And the foolish said to the wise, 'Give us some of your oil, for our lamps are going out.' But the wise answered, saying, 'No, lest there should not be enough for us and you; but go rather to those who sell, and buy for yourselves.' And while they went to buy, the bridegroom came, and those who were ready went in with him to the wedding; and the door was shut.

"Afterward the other virgins came also, saying, 'Lord, Lord, open to us!' But he answered and said, 'Assuredly, I say to you, I do not know you.'

"Watch therefore, for you know neither the day nor the hour in which the Son of Man is coming."

The ten virgins represent Christians and their purity. For example we read in 2 Corinthians 11:2:

"I am jealous for you with a godly jealousy. I promised you to one husband, to Christ, so that I might present you as a pure virgin to him."

The bridegroom represents Jesus Christ at his second coming and the wedding represents the Kingdom of God.

As the foolish virgins realised their predicament they desperately asked the wise virgins for some of their oil. The wise virgins responded by telling them they could not share their oil because they would then run out of it themselves. The foolish virgins hurriedly went off to the town to buy oil but while they were gone the bridegroom came and went and the door to the wedding was locked shut.

There are many valuable lessons to learn from this parable. The one I would like to highlight though is this: we cannot as Christians rely on other people's 'oil' to fill our lamp to light our own path. We need our own oil!

The oil here represents the Holy Spirit and our relationship with Him. The lamp is the eye. Jesus said: *"Your eye is a lamp that provides light for your body. When your eye is good, your whole body is filled with light. But when it is bad, your body is filled with darkness."* (Luke 11:34)

The Holy Spirit then must fill our 'lamps' and flood us with His light. Just as I saw in my vision, the end time saints had such an indwelling of the Holy Spirit in their lives, such a relationship with Christ, that it was evident and visible through their physical eyes.

It is only a deep relationship with God through Jesus Christ empowered by the Holy Spirit that can brighten our path to see the way through the utter darkness of this world. If we don't have a personal relationship with the Lord then we will become totally lost in the end time darkness.

There's Still Time

Friends, it's really time we found our own oil, our own relationship with the Lord! We can't rely on our friend's oil, or our pastor's oil, or on a top-up of oil at church on Sunday. These are valid but they are not sufficient. We all need our own oil direct from the Holy Spirit.

It is time we climbed off the fence of indifference. It is time we fully said goodbye to the world and wholly embrace Christ. If we don't we will be lost in the dark. The scriptures tell us that if we are friends of the world we are enemies of God (James 4:4).

Friends, let's today draw near to God in relationship with Him, and as the scriptures promise, he will draw near in relationship with us.

"Therefore submit to God. Resist the devil and he will flee from you. Draw near to God and He will draw near to you. Cleanse your hands, you sinners; and purify your hearts, you double-minded. Lament and mourn and weep! Let your laughter be turned to mourning and your joy to gloom. Humble yourselves in the sight of the Lord, and He will lift you up." (James 4:7-10)

Friends, it is time to get right with God; that clock around our neck is ticking. Let's not waste another moment living a mediocre lifestyle. But let us react as King David did. When David, who knew God and walked with him, realised his desperate spiritual condition he cried out in urgency of soul:

"Create in me a clean heart, O God, and renew a right, persevering, and steadfast spirit within me. Cast me not away from Your presence and take not Your Holy Spirit from me. Restore to me the joy of Your salvation and uphold me with a willing spirit. Then will I teach

transgressors Your ways, and sinners shall be converted and return to You." (Psalm 51:10)

Let's do it now. Let's not delay for our salvation is much nearer now than when we first believed. Let's resist the devil now when there is still time.

"The night is far spent, the day is at hand. Therefore let us cast off the works of darkness, and let us put on the armour of light. Let us walk properly, as in the day, not in revelry and drunkenness, not in lewdness and lust, not in strife and envy. But put on the Lord Jesus Christ, and make no provision for the flesh, to fulfill its lusts." (Romans 13:12-14)

Friends, there will come a day soon when the warning blast of the trumpet I heard in my vision suddenly stops sounding. The warning will be over, end time events will overtake the earth, and after that the books will be opened, including the Book of Life, and anyone's name not found written in there will be lost forever (Revelation 20:11-15). There will be no time to repent, no time left to draw near to God.

Let us then not be left lost in the dark like the foolish virgins! But rather let us heed the urging of the apostle Paul:

"Awake, you who sleep,
Arise from the dead,
And Christ will give you light." (Ephesians 5:14)

Let us walk as children of the light, having no fellowship with the unfruitful works of darkness (Ephesians 5:8-11).

Let us embrace Christ now while it is still day.

There's still time!

Trumpet Blast Warning — An end time prophetic wake up call — Available direct from **www.trumpetblastwarning.co.uk** or from Amazon paperback or Kindle and in selected bookstores.

After experiencing a dramatic wake up call Jason Carter began a period of intensive research about the connection between end-time Bible prophecies and contemporary events on the world stage.

The results of his intensive investigations are startling.

In Trumpet Blast Warning you will discover how

- minds are being manipulated through mass media propaganda
- freedoms and democracy are being subtly eroded
- national sovereignties are being replaced by a one world government
- human catastrophes are not always as 'accidental' as they seem
- technology and surveillance are being used to control and oppress
- the Antichrist spirit is intensifying all over the earth
- the world is gearing up for the climactic events of history

Unless the trumpet is sounded no one will get ready. Jason Carter's book sounds an unequivocal trumpet blast warning and rallies everyone to be prepared.

Truly, the countdown to the Apocalypse has begun.

What others are saying

This book is not for those who live in their own reality bubble, it is a shocking fact about those bankers and corrupt politicians who are calling for a New World government. You will find further evidence of Presidents and senior politicians attending secret meetings around the world where they engage in occult practices. If you think God does not exist then surely you must acknowledge that the devil does exist after reading this book. Highly recommended for those who have an open mind and value their freedom. — *Michael (Amazon review)*
★★★★★

This is eye-opening, to say the least! If you have any inkling of what is happening in the US and worldwide today, this book confirms it! Simply awesome! Are you prepared for what's to come? I suggest everyone, Christian, athiest, agnostic...EVERYONE needs to read it! — *Pamela*

A compelling book for the epoch in which we all live. This book will create a reaction within each reader who will weigh the narrative that unfolds before them as either truth or conspiracy. Either way it will demand a response, it did with me and woke me up out of a deep sleep. — *John (Amazon review)*
★★★★★

Help to get the message out –
like, share & *follow*
Trumpet Blast Warning
on Facebook or Twitter

www.facebook.com/trumpetblastwarning

www.twitter.com/NewProphecyBook

To order further copies of
Trumpet Blast Warning or *Beyond Earthly Realms* visit
www.trumpetblastwarning.co.uk

Printed in Great Britain
by Amazon

42253399R00089